COACHING BASKETBALL'S SCRAMBLE DEFENSE

Jim Larranaga

COACHES ≡CHOICE™

ISBN: 1-58518-322-9

Library of Congress Number: 00-108302

Book Layout & Diagrams: Jennifer Bokelmann / Jeanne Hamilton

Cover Design: Paul Lewis

Coaches Choice
P.O. Box 1828
Monterey, CA 93942
www.coacheschoiceweb.com

DEDICATION

To Liz, Jay, and Jon.

ACKNOWLEDGEMENTS

There are many people I would like to thank for being there for me throughout the years. I would also like to express my appreciation to those who helped with this project.

First of all, I want to thank my wife, Liz, who is always encouraging me to "go for it." My two sons, Jay and Jon, who have given me more proud moments than any Dad could ask for. My brothers, Greg and Bob, who got me started on a life of fun-filled basketball. My coaches, Jack Curran, Joe Mullaney, Dave Gavitt and Terry Holland, who brought me into college coaching, and for sharing their knowledge with me. I want to thank Dr. Bob Rotella for helping me to dream big.

I want to also thank my secretary, Carolyn Marsh, for putting up with me each day and especially for putting this project together. I am forever grateful to Dr. Alan Merten, President of George Mason University, and Tom O'Connor, Director of Athletics, for giving me the opportunity to build a championship caliber program and for having faith that it could be done.

And special thanks to all my players and assistants who contributed greatly throughout my career.

— J.L.

CONTENTS

INTRODUCTION

I grew up in New York City. My two older brothers, Greg and Bob, introduced me to the game of basketball when I was eight-years-old. They were my first coaches. During the next ten years, and throughout high school and college, I developed a true love for the game and decided I wanted to be a college coach one day.

I had the distinct pleasure of playing for Jack Curran, the winningest coach in the State of New York's history, at Archbishop Molloy High School. Coach Curran is the best teacher I have ever had in any subject. His passion for teaching was passed along to me during my high school days. As a great teacher and motivator, Curran always stressed the fundamentals. He was *totally committed to excellence* and made sure his teams performed that way. *"Practice does not make perfect, perfect practice makes perfect",* Coach Curran would preach daily. His practices were always demanding and competitive. More importantly, they were fun. Practice each day included drill after drill on every aspect of basketball fundamentals. We were always in fantastic shape, driven by our coach and his encouragement to be the best. When we took the court we *knew* we were going to win. By the time I graduated, all five players in my senior class were recruited and went to Division I schools on scholarships. Our four-year record was 85-5, including two undefeated seasons and two New York City Championships, in my freshman and sophomore years.

I was fortunate enough to be recruited and offered a scholarship to play at Providence College. The head coach, Joe Mullaney, had just completed his tenth consecutive 20-win season. He was a cool, calm and collected coach who never lost his poise under pressure. However, after my sophomore year at Providence, Coach Mullaney left the Friars to become the head coach of the Los Angeles Lakers. He went from coaching me to coaching Jerry West. He must have enjoyed that.

Providence decided to hire a very popular former assistant, Dave Gavitt, to replace Coach Mullaney. Coach Gavitt was skilled in every aspect of college coaching. He was an outstanding recruiter, teacher, strategist and political figure. His incredible career has spanned four decades. He coached Providence College to eight consecutive 20-win seasons, and reached five NCAA Tournaments, including a trip to the 1973 Final Four. In 1979, he founded the Big East Conference and was the conference's first commissioner. He was named coach of the 1980 U.S. Olympic Team and probably would have led the team to a gold medal had The United States not boycotted the 1980 Olympics. From 1990 to 1994, he served as Chief Executive Officer and Vice Chairman of the Board of the Boston Celtics. He is now the Chairman of the Board of the Basketball Hall of Fame. He has had a big impact on my coaching career, and for this I will be forever grateful.

After a most successful college basketball career, I was drafted by the Detroit Pistons of the NBA. As a sixth-round draft pick, the odds were stacked against me, but I was determined to make it in the NBA. Shortly before leaving for the Pistons' training camp,   I was offered a full-time assistant coaching position by Terry Holland, head coach at Davidson College in North Carolina. The offer really excited me. The NBA had always been a dream of mine, but so had coaching college basketball. This decision would affect the rest of my life. Rather than forcing me to choose, Coach Holland allowed me to try out for the Pistons. If I made the team, I would begin my NBA career; if I got cut, well, I would be on my way to Davidson with my wife, Liz.

Although the tryouts were great, my experience ended on a sour note. I pulled a muscle in my thigh during the last few days of camp and could not continue. So ended my NBA hopes. In September of 1971, I accepted Coach Terry Holland's offer and became a Division I assistant at age 21.

In my first three years at Davidson, we won three Southern Conference regular-season championships. College coaching was everything I thought it would be and more. I started out believing I knew a lot about the game of basketball, and for a 21-year-old, I probably did. But as the youngest full-time assistant in Division I, what I would learn during the next 28 years was far more than I could have ever imagined. I owe a big thanks to Terry Holland for bringing me into such a great profession, and many thanks to my coaches Jack Curran, Joe Mullaney, and Dave Gavitt for preparing me so well.

Like many Division I head coaches who have enjoyed success, the credit should go to my assistant coaches as well. I may be luckier than many. I have hired and had the pleasure of working with some outstanding assistant coaches who have contributed to my coaching philosophy. Many of them have gone on to fame and fortune. They are:

Marc Iavaroni – Assistant Coach, Miami Heat

Jim Powell – Lead Scout, Indiana Pacers

Brian Ellerbe – Head Coach, University of Michigan

Ricky Stokes – Head Coach, Virginia Tech

Jeff Schneider – Head Coach, Cal Poly San Luis Obispo

Steve Merfeld – Head Coach, Hampton University

Jamie Angeli – Assistant Coach, UCLA

Tom Sorboro – Assistant Coach, University of Michigan

Charlie Gross – Head Coach, Wisconsin La Crosse

Joe Huber – Assistant Coach, Luther College

Anthony Solomon – Assistant Coach, Notre Dame University

Arthur Jackson – One-on-One Basketball - Washington, D.C.

Stan Heath – Assistant Coach, Michigan State University

Jerry Francis – Assistant Coach, University of Houston

Reggie Rankin – Assistant Coach, University of Nebraska

Jamie Kachmarik – Assistant Coach, College of William & Mary

Keith Noftz – Assistant Coach, Bowling Green State University

Jeff Westlund – Assistant Coach, Bethel College

Todd Rinehart – Assistant Coach, University of Denver

Mike Gillian – Assistant Coach, George Mason University

Bill Courtney – Assistant Coach, George Mason University

Derek Kellogg – Assistant Coach, University of Memphis

Most of these young coaches got their start with me at Bowling Green. They helped me develop my style and philosophy. Subsequently, many of them have enjoyed success at other schools. I follow their careers closely. I feel in some way a part of their success. I hope they feel the same way.

As I begin my 30th season in college coaching, I am reminded of one of my brother Bob's favorite quotes from the great Chinese philosopher Confucius, "Choose a job you love and you will never have to work a day in your life." I made that choice in 1971, and I am glad I did.

— Jim Larranaga

1

SCRAMBLE PHILOSOPHY

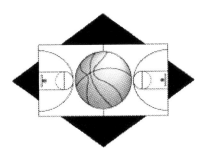

I learned during the course of my coaching career that it is very important to establish a philosophy. Your *philosophy* is basically a sum of all your convictions. It's who you are. It's what you stand for. It is what others perceive of you. But most importantly, it is how you see yourself and what you believe in.

I believe that your philosophy must be more than just a basketball philosophy; it must be a philosophy about life. You must teach your players how they can be successful no matter what their goal or challenge. In other words, emphasize being the best that you can be at whatever you do.

At George Mason, our basketball philosophy is simple; it is based on three very basic principles. These three principles are fundamental qualities that we expect everyone associated with our program to understand and live by:

- To approach everything with a *positive attitude*

- To demonstrate a *total and unconditional commitment* to our program

- To do things in a *first-class manner*

WHAT IS A POSITIVE ATTITUDE?

Life is 10 percent what *happens* to you, and 90 percent how you *react* to it. The most consistent quality you see in the successful person is a positive attitude. The successful person learns to overcome obstacles and to treat adversity as a part of the process of becoming successful. A positive attitude includes a genuine enthusiasm for life and a commitment to achieving one's goals.

WHAT IS A TOTAL AND UNCONDITIONAL COMMITMENT?

The essence of commitment is the desire to succeed, the determination to reach your goals, and the discipline to perform even when you do not feel like performing. The ability to perform the most meaningless task "well", to pay close attention to every detail, and to do so honestly and with integrity is the sign of commitment. In other words, commitment involves making whatever sacrifice is necessary to obtain your goals and committing yourself totally and without reservation. Only when you make that kind of commitment can you truly be successful.

WHAT IS CLASS?

You must be proud of who you are. Pride in oneself is developed through the consistent effort of doing things in a first-class manner. Class is who you are, the way you project yourself. Class cannot be bought or sold. It is the way you act, the way you dress, the way you speak, the way you live. Class is doing things correctly. Class is the attitude and commitment to "being the best that you can be" in thought, word and deed. We emphasize these qualities to our players each and every day.

BASKETBALL IS A SIMPLE GAME

Simply put, basketball is a game of fundamentals. It basically comes down to passing, catching, screening, shooting, rebounding, and a whole lot of defense. Most coaches emphasize offense because it is fun and exciting. The players enjoy it, and it is easy to teach. In my coaching experience, however, it is defense that wins championships. That prescription for success was continually emphasized to me throughout my playing and coaching days.

Why is defense so important? Ask Bill Russell, who led his Boston Celtic team to 11 World Championships in 13 years. Ask John Wooden, the greatest basketball coach in college history, who won seven consecutive NCAA titles and 10 total during his legendary career at UCLA. Even ask Michael Jordan, the greatest offensive player in the history of the game, who led his Chicago Bulls' teams to six World Championships. They all agree that to win championships, a team must focus on the defensive end of the floor.

Bill Russell dominated the NBA with his shot blocking, rebounding, and defensive intimidation. His Celtic teams were recognized as the best pressing team in professional basketball.

John Wooden's reign at UCLA was highly acclaimed by all who followed college basketball. His 2-2-1 full court press became "the defense of the 60's and 70's." (Note: like the Scramble Defense will be in the first decade of the new millenium).

Michael Jordan, in his book, *For Love of the Game – My Story*, said that the champion New York Knicks of the early 70's were similar to his first three championship teams with the Bulls because both Coach Red Holzman and Coach Phil Jackson emphasized defense. "I decided I wanted to be recognized as a player who could influence the game at either end of the floor. Defense was my way of separating myself from other great players, like Larry Bird and Magic Johnson. I took great pride in being able to shut down my man and also play great team defense," said Jordan. He also feels that defense is why the Bulls won six championships despite the change of personnel. Jordan says, "Give me guys with heart and brains and strong fundamentals. No matter what happens in the game of basketball, those elements will always determine success." Jordan, like Bill Russell and John Wooden, believed that a team could only win championships if it played great team defense.

Why defense? The simplest way to explain it is to ask yourself how many games would you win if your team always shot 50 percent or better? If that were the case, you should win almost every game. However, the fact of the matter is very few teams are able to shoot 50 percent on a regular basis. What is going to happen when you shoot less than 50 percent or even less than 40 percent? Will you still win? Great teams have found a way to win even when they are not shooting the ball well.

This is particularly true when you are on the road and playing in a relatively hostile environment. The opponent has the home-court advantage. Its players are familiar with their surroundings. They shoot the ball better at home, and your team's players don't shoot quite as well on the road. Do you concede the victory? No! The answer is...you dig down deep and play great defense. You force the opponent into a lower shooting percentage or more turnovers than they are used to committing. Your defensive rebounding limits them to one shot, and you still control the game. Your offense may be great some nights, and on those nights you will probably win. But it is when your offense is not at its best that your true test occurs. This instance is when all championship teams know that defense wins championships.

Defense is hard work. Those players who will succeed are those who learn that it takes extra effort to perform at your best. It takes extra effort to succeed. You cannot perform at your best without hard work. You must enjoy the effort. Yes, it is work but it is also fun. I repeat... *WORK IS FUN.* We stress to our players each and every day that they must improve. You are either getting better or getting worse. No one stays the same. Improving is fun.

GOAL SETTING

The key to improvement is goal setting. You must know what your goals are and work toward them daily. You must concentrate not on the *result*, but on the *process*. Focus on the present, not on the past or future. Focus on the task at hand. You must visualize yourself accomplishing these goals or they will never become a reality. We believe that all things are created twice:

- *Mentally* – You must see it in your mind first.

- *Physically* – Once you see it in your mind, then you can create it.

Our offense begins with defense. We create easy baskets by forcing turnovers. Our players are willing and eager to play great defense because they know that a good defensive play will often lead to a lay-up. This attitude is part of our coaching philosophy. We expect our players to understand our philosophy and to adhere to it at all times, at both ends of the court.

AFFIRMATIONS

We play defense with a positive attitude, a total commitment to hard work, and we will do it in a first-class manner. We have five defensive affirmations to which we are totally committed. These five affirmations are the first five steps to having a successful defensive-minded basketball team under game conditions.

They are:

- We...pressure the ball.

- We...deny all passes.

- We...prevent penetration.

- We...communicate and help.

- We...rebound and run.

We are *totally committed* to pressure defense. In other words, we pressure the ball at all times. Our players know what is expected of them. They know that if their man has the ball, they should be all over him putting as much pressure as their physical skills allow. While the man with the ball is being pressured, the men without the ball are being denied. We want to contest every pass, every dribble, every shot, and every rebound. We expect our team to be the aggressor. We do not want to wait to see what the offense does. We want to create the action. We believe that players perform at their best when they feel they are dictating what is happening on the floor – whether it be on offense or defense.

2

HISTORY OF THE SCRAMBLE

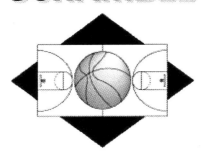

In the fall of 1996, Ben Braun, the great head men's basketball coach at the University of California–Berkeley, made a profound statement that changed my career and helped me win two conference championships, as well as two Coach-of-the-Year awards in the last three seasons...but more about that later.

THE BEGINNING

The genesis of the Scramble Defense began when I was an assistant coach to Terry Holland at the University of Virginia. I helped coach the Cavalier team, led by Ralph Sampson and Jeff Lamp, to a 29-4 record and a trip to the NCAA Final Four. That was the best half-court offensive team with which I have ever been associated.

In the fall of 1981, it was a different story. With the season quickly approaching, our staff was faced with a new look. Jeff Lamp and Lee Raker, two super shooters, had graduated. Although their long-range shooting would be missed, we were excited about the speed and quickness in our lineup that would complement Ralph Sampson, a great shot blocker.

The "Scramble Defense" began as a series of compromises when our coaching staff at Virginia was attempting to utilize our speed and quickness in the backcourt and our size in the front court. At first, Terry Holland, the brilliant young head coach of Virginia, was committed to man-to-man defense. During our ten years together, three years at Davidson and seven years at Virginia, Holland's teams played 97 percent man-to-man. However, Holland always adjusted to his personnel.

In 1981-82 with a very fast team returning, the coaching staff was convinced we needed to press. A zone press was a natural choice, leaving Sampson deep to defend the basket. But Coach Holland wanted to match up and assign greater responsibility to each individual. With two jet-quick guards, Othell Wilson and Ricky Stokes, we had the ability to put man-to-man pressure on any point guard in the country. With Ralph Sampson we had a one-man zone. Against any press, straight man-to-man, or zone, your opponent can either (a) run a set press attack, (b) clear out, or (c) set screens and force switches. What we needed was a defense that combined both man and zone principles. We were looking for a defense that incorporated:

- Man-to-man with match-up responsibilities.

- The ability to trap.

- Traits that made it difficult to recognize.

- Features so it could be utilized as either a full-court or half-court defense.

By borrowing some of the concepts from my high school coach and some concepts from Dean Smith's North Carolina run-and-jump defense, we created the "Scramble Defense". It became the key element in Virginia's league-leading steals and scoring average, a regular season ACC Championship, and it's number one national ranking for a large portion of the season. We won 30 games that year, including a 15-point win over North Carolina. Had Othell Wilson not been injured in the ACC Tournament's first round, the history of college basketball might be different. We lost that year to North Carolina in the ACC Tournament Finals, and, still without Wilson, lost a heartbreaker to UAB in the NCAA Tournament Sweet 16. North Carolina went on to win the National Championship. Michael Jordan's game winning shot against Georgetown sealed the victory for the Tarheels. I am convinced that Othell Wilson's injury kept us from winning a national championship. However, the "Scramble Defense", which we had used so successfully throughout the season, had become an integral part of our defensive strategy.

Two years later, with Othell Wilson, Rick Carlisle, and Ricky Stokes leading the way, and without Ralph Sampson, Virginia was back in the Final Four. This time we were propelled by the defense that has become a major part of my coaching philosophy – *"THE SCRAMBLE"*.

THE KEY

In 1986, I became the head men's basketball coach at Bowling Green State University. During my first ten years, we used "The Scramble" sporadically throughout each game. However, in 1996 that all changed. Ben Braun, then the coach of Eastern Michigan University, left to become the head men's basketball coach of the University of California at Berkeley. Coach Braun and I competed against each other for 10 years. I had the utmost respect for him and his teams. When he left the Mid-American Conference to coach the Golden Bears, I gave him a call to congratulate him. I also wanted to pick his brain and ask him what it was like to play against my Bowling Green teams. I wondered what we could do to improve ourselves.

That conversation proved to be *the key* moment in my coaching career. Coach Braun said, "You need to scramble more." He said that during his 10 years of coaching against my teams, the one thing that bothered him most was when we scrambled. "The more you do it, the better you'll do it. The better you do it, the more you *can* do it. I think if you use it all the time, you'll win a Mid-American Conference Championship," Coach Braun proclaimed.

WERE WE READY?

Were we ready to make a total commitment to pressure defense? If so, we needed to take another step with our man-to-man defense. For 10 years, we had played basic man-to-man, ball-you-basket defense. It was consistent with our man-to-man defense from my days at The University of Virginia. We knew that if we were totally convinced that pressure defense was what we were going to do, then it had to begin with our man-to-man. During my years in the Midwest, I became very aware of the super job Dick Bennett, the head men's basketball coach at Wisconsin, had done at Wisconsin-Stevens Point and also at Wisconsin-Green Bay. I began to study his "up-the-line and on-the line", man-to-man defensive concepts that he used most effectively at Stevens Point.

In this defense, Coach Bennett emphasized putting great pressure on both the ball and the entry pass. Each defender was expected to deny his man the ball. The more I learned, the more I liked what I saw. I called Coach Bennett and asked him a series of questions that he was kind enough to answer. By the time I got off the phone, I knew we had found the perfect half-court, man-to-man defense to complement our full-court and half-court Scramble Defense. We were very excited to implement our plan.

THE TEST

Going into the 1996-97 season, my staff and I were committed to playing The Scramble on every made basket and free throw for an entire game and season. The results were amazing. In our first game of the season, we were on the road to face Lefty Driesell's James Madison team. They were very talented and a little bigger than us. We jumped out to a 13-0 lead. We led 33-13 with just under ten minutes to play in the first half. The Scramble worked to perfection. Since we were their opening game, they hadn't been able to scout us. James Madison couldn't prepare for what we were doing. They did make a run to end the first half, but we exploded in the second half. We eventually won the game and at one point led by 30 points. We passed the first test, but how would it work against a bigger and more powerful team?

Two games later, we faced Purdue, the three-time defending Big Ten Champion. Gene Keady's teams were always well prepared and very physical. We were very small. Our starting line up had only one player over 6'5". That night at Purdue, we forced 28 turnovers and beat them on their home court, 85-82, only their second non-conference home loss in the 90's. We scrambled both half-court and full-court, from start to finish, on every score. The pressure was relentless. We contested every pass, every dribble, every shot, and every rebound. Our players loved it. Every mistake converted into a fast break, jump shot, lay-up, or dunk. Every mistake late in the game magnified itself. You could see our confidence growing and our opponent's confidence dwindling as the game neared its end. Led by Antonio Daniels, now of the World Champion San Antonio Spurs, and my son, Jay, Bowling Green went on to win our first ever regular season Mid-American Conference Championship. We set a school record for conference victories (13) and tied the school record for victories in a season (22). Four of our starting five were among the top seven in the conference for steals. And we averaged over 20 forced turnovers per game. The Scramble worked.

Ben Braun had been prophetic. The Scramble had led us to our first regular season championship, but, for me, it wouldn't be the last.

WOULD IT WORK AT GEORGE MASON?

On April 1, 1997, I became the head men's basketball coach at George Mason University in Fairfax, Virginia. George Mason had suffered through seven straight losing seasons. But within two years and with the Scramble Defense in place, we took George Mason to its first ever regular season CAA Championship, and its second ever CAA Tournament Championship and NCAA Tournament appearance. We led our league in forced turnovers at 20 per game. We set the school record for conference victories (13). We led our league in scoring and in steals. We were developing a style of play that was recognized by every coach, player and fan around our conference. George Mason played hard. "They pressure the ball as well as anyone." That's what people were saying.

The awards started to filter in. George Evans, our go-to guy on offense, was named the conference player-of-the-year, the defensive player-of-the-year, first- team all conference and first-team all district. Jason Miskiri, our point guard, was named first-team all conference and first-team all district. For my contribution, I was named the Colonial Athletic Association Coach-of-the-Year, the State of Virginia Coach-of-the-Year, and the NABC District Coach-of-the-Year. The recognition was very rewarding, since we had come such a long way in a relatively short period of time.

Now that we have completed four full seasons of being totally committed to   The Scramble (one season at Bowling Green and three at George Mason), we believe that it will propel us to many conference championships. I have observed several NBA coaches (e.g., George Karl of the Milwaukee Bucks, Larry Brown of the Philadelphia 76ers, and Rick Pitino, formerly at Kentucky, and now of the Boston Celtics) who have enjoyed tremendous success with their particular style and approach to pressure defense. In fact, forcing turnovers and getting easy baskets in the open court make The Scramble a lethal weapon.

Keep in mind that The Scramble can work effectively for all types of teams. For example, the quicker the players are on your team, the more you can extend The Scramble. However, if you are not the quicker team, you can still scramble effectively by scrambling more at the half-court level and shortening your rotations.

The one thing we want our players to believe is that they can outwork the opponent. We are committed to working hard year-round. We lift weights as a team twelve months of the year. We have intense individual workouts, plus agilities and conditioning during the pre-season. We want our players to believe that they are the hardest working team in our conference and in the country. We believe that the greatest compliment that anyone can give our team is that "they play hard all the time."

3

MAN-TO-MAN DEFENSE

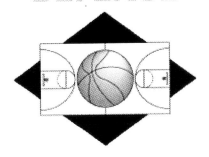

sk yourself this question, "What separates us from all other teams?" At George Mason, we
know the answer to this question – The Scramble. But before reviewing The Scramble, however, an explanation of our man-to-man defense can be helpful. Knowing how our man-to-man
and The Scramble complement each other can enhance a better understanding of how we effectively employ The Scramble. In essence, our man-to-man defense has become part of The
Scramble because it sets the stage for all of our defensive pressure throughout each game.

UP THE LINE, ON THE LINE

As I mentioned earlier, at one time our man-to-man defense was your basic "ball,-you,-basket"
defense. We were pretty conservative and believed that you had to first and foremost stay between the ball and the basket, and between your man and the basket. We believed then, and still
believe now, that the key to great defense is preventing penetration. At the University of Virginia,
we wanted to have a physical presence between the man with the ball and the basket. We expected our defense to prevent dribble penetration. We felt that if we stayed between the ball
and the basket, we would be in a great rebounding position and could limit our opponent to one
shot. This philosophy is very sound and can be extremely effective. However, we found that
particular approach has some definite drawbacks.

For example, when playing between your man and the basket, the defense concedes every
pass on the perimeter and into the low post. Your opponent can run it's man-to-man offense and
generally get the shots it's looking for. Your opponent can execute the same offense it uses in
every game and every day in practice. We believe that if you play a good team, you will eventually
give up some easy baskets and allow your opponent to get into a good rhythm. When your opponent gets into a good rhythm, the opposing players' confidence will grow.

Most shots players take are rhythm shots. In other words, they are stepping into the shot, right then left, or left then right. It is like dancing to music. The footwork repeats itself. Good offense also requires rhythm. For example, look at the Flex offense. The Flex offense looks first for a baseline cutter, then a shooter coming off a down screen, then a new cutter and a new shooter. It's the same look each time. Also, review the Motion offense. Motion offense asks the offensive players to read the defense and then move accordingly. First a down screen, then a backscreen. You have a screener and a man using the screen working together. They are "dancing." The same situations repeat themselves, possession after possession.

The point is, the best way to stop these offenses is to disrupt the normal rhythm. Switch! Deny! Keep them from making the next pass. Then, they will react to you. Instead of getting their normal shots in the course of running their offense, they must freelance. They will not get a shot in their normal rhythm. Sometimes, even a good shot will be missed because the player subconsciously realizes that this shot is not one the team is looking for. It is out of the normal offense.

WHAT DO I DO NOW?

If the other team gets into a good rhythm on offense, what should you do?

When you reach this point in a game, every coach begins to consider these options. If the other team is scoring regularly, should I:

- call a time out and make adjustments to our man-to-man?

- change our defense and possibly use a zone?

- change my personnel and hope our subs can do a better job?

- stick with what we are doing and hope our opponent misses?

The answer is not always obvious. In fact, based on my experience as a head coach, at this point in a game my three assistants will each have a different opinion about what strategy we should employ. Each option usually has its own merits. Which one should be selected?

Since 1996, when we made the commitment to pressure defense, the answer has always been the same. Now we believe that the best way to defend your opponent is to attack him. Do not let your opponent run their offense. Keep the opponent off balance. Make them react to you. We want to put extreme pressure on the ball handler and his pass receivers. We deny every entry pass into the offense. This strategy creates an entirely different atmosphere on the court. No longer are the offensive players in their comfort zone. No longer are we allowing the other team to execute their half-court offense and waiting for them to shoot. Now we take the initiative. We eliminate the most common opportunities our opponent sees each game. We take away reversal passes and keep the ball on one side of the floor. We limit the number of touches a good post player will get during the course of the game.

We teach our players to gain a numerical advantage on every possession. We want all five defensive players on the ball-side of the floor. We want to defend our opponent five-on-three.

Rarely do we see an offense that has more than three players on the ball-side. Good spacing requires the offense to spread out. However, we coach our defense not to spread out because it allows good dribble-penetration opportunities for the ball handler.

Our emphasis is on doing a great job of playing on-the-ball defense and forcing our opponent to the outside. Once the ball is on the side of the court, we have five defenders to defend three offensive players. We have two players in perfect *help* position. We remind our team that if our opponent tries to penetrate our defense, we must prevent penetration by helping each other. That does not mean the pressure is off, simply because someone penetrated on the dribble, drew the help defender, and completed a pass. In fact, our defense must react quickly and again apply pressure, this time to a wing or forward. Get some pressure on him and make him adjust. Get him out of his comfort zone.

While we are applying great pressure to the ball handler and his pass receiver, the opposing coach is often instructing his players to execute. One of the worst feelings a coach can have is when his team makes a bad pass, and the defense converts the bad pass into a turnover, a fast break, a lay-up, or a dunk. Something is wrong. "EXECUTE," he yells. He begs his team to run the offense. The beauty of this scenario is that the defense can anticipate every pass. The defense is well prepared and knows what the offense is looking for. By disrupting the natural flow of offense, the defensive team gains a tremendous psychological advantage.

By forcing 20 turnovers a game, we know we are going to get more shots at our basket than our opponent. If both teams shoot approximately the same percentage, we will win. We gain a clear statistical advantage. We average 60 shots per game, our opponent attempts only 52. In league play, our opponent's average points-per-game allowed is 65. However, we average 74 points per game in the conference. Why? Or better still, how? The answer is simple. We lead the league in scoring and field-goal percentage because our pressure defense creates easy baskets – lots of them.

When we play defense we have a great physical presence between the ball and our man. We also have a much more powerful ally. We now have a great *"psychological"* advantage. We have a presence that can be felt on every pass, every dribble, every rebound, and every shot. The results are relatively staggering.

If you employ The Scramble, your opponent has to prepare for you differently. Because most teams seldom face The Scramble, they have to spend each practice session leading up to the game trying to prepare for it. Their normal practice routine is disrupted. They will spend two or three days preparing their offense against a defense we have spent months and years preparing. In response to the pressure that they will encounter from The Scramble, the opposing coach has to warn his players of the constant danger and how careful they have to be with the ball. As a result, before the game even begins, you have them reacting to you. From your team's perspective, there can be no better preparation!

Pressure defense does have its tradeoffs. At times, when your defense breaks down or is slow to react, you will give up some easy baskets. The difference between these situations and when you are playing conservative man-to-man is that your opponent's offense will not have rhythm. Any basket your opponent scores will not be the result of a well-executed play, but due to a breakdown in your defense. You have control over this factor. A little adjustment in your defense on the next possession, and that same play may result in a steal.

In teaching our man-to-man defense, we begin with full-court ball pressure. We play nose-on-the-ball (refer to Chapter 7) and expect our defender to *turn* the dribbler three times before crossing the mid-court line. When the defender on the ball is given an objective (e.g., turning the dribbler three times before mid-court), it gives him a clear way to measure how he is doing. If the ball handler is able to easily advance the ball and is changing directions only once or twice, we know and he knows that there is not enough pressure being applied. Each of our point guards is drilled every day on applying ball pressure. They take great pride in turning the dribbler at least three times.

Once we have clearly established our on-the-ball pressure, we look closely at the pressure on the wings as the first pass receivers. We tell our wing defenders to deny. In fact, the defense is required to yell "deny, deny, deny", as their man attempts to receive the first pass. His mechanics are very specific. You must have your *lead hand* in the passing lane between your man and the ball. You must have your hand "on the line." Your body position is "up the line." This directive means that your body is three to six feet *closer to the ball than your man*. Simply put, you should be one or two steps off your man in the passing lane, denying him the ball (refer to Diagrams 3-1 and 3-2).

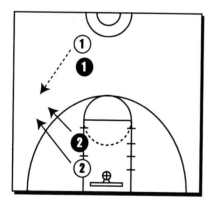

Diagram 3-1.

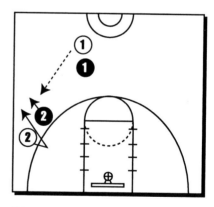

Diagram 3-2.

Diagrams 3-1 and 3-2 illustrate the best position for denying your man, while helping your teammate guard the dribbler. We encourage our players to constantly fake at the dribbler if he tries to attack the gap. The danger of this position is the possibility of a backdoor cut for an easy lay-up. That is why it is imperative to get great pressure on the ball and good help from the help-side defenders. We work on this every day (refer to Chapter 7 for the wing-deny and shell drill). Since most teams are not experienced at timing a perfect backdoor cut and pass, we believe the danger is limited to one or two plays per game. We can accept this limitation because we will force far more mistakes during the course of the game.

Our low-post defense is critical to our defensive pressure. How you play the low-post will determine who helps and how you react to the post feed or the baseline drive.

Our first consideration, before the season begins, is how many low-post players can score effectively if we let them catch the ball. If the answer is relatively few, then we strongly consider a half to three-quarters straddle in the post and play him straight up on a post feed. However, if we determine that many of the post men we will face will probably score on us on a regular basis if we let them catch the post-pass easily, we tell our low-post defenders to front and absolutely deny them the ball at all cost. If this is the case, we want our opponent to have to *lob* the ball to get it inside. We then teach our help defenders to be in a position to either: steal the pass; take the charge when he catches it; trap; or block the shot. If we have good pressure on the passer, this play is not easy and will often lead to turnovers.

Should a low-post man be too big to front, then our last option is to straddle and play behind on the post feed. We will *double team* with the nearest man to the middle of the floor and rotate. We fully expect to force the post man into a difficult decision and likely, a turnover. Frankly, finding an open man with your back to the basket is a great skill that few big men have developed.

RUN AND STUN

In the NBA, all good offensive low-post scorers get double teamed. The defense forces the post player to kick it out and shoot a perimeter shot. Coaches in the NBA believe this is a better percentage play than to allow a good scorer a one-on-one opportunity. We happen to agree. Therefore, we attack the ball in the low-post. We call this the "run and stun." It means that on any pass or drive that may lead to an easy basket, we trap the ball handler.

Our post defense also plays a critical role in helping perimeter players defend baseline drives. Since we are forcing the ball handler to the outside, it stands to reason that we will get beat on the baseline from time to time. We instruct and drill our post men to give plenty of help and eventually trap any player who drives baseline as he nears the three-second lane. Again, we believe that this is not a great position to have the ball in a double team, with the dribble now dead. All five defenders run to the lane and anticipate a shot or pass. We practice this situation in our shell drill (refer to Chapter 7) every day. We also use the term "run and stun" to describe this situation. We want everyone to understand that the ball is getting closer and closer to the basket on either the dribble or the pass, and we must prevent an easy score.

SWITCHING

Having established our man-to-man pressure, we must be able to handle specific situations designed to relieve the pressure by the offense. In order to keep our help-side defense in position, we switch on any perimeter-on-perimeter screen away from the ball. We will also switch on any post-to-post screen. By doing this, we almost always have one perimeter and one post man in help-side position. It is important to drill this daily.

Many teams like to flash a man to the high post and create a high-low situation. We always deny the flash, since he is basically a reversal pass receiver. We adjust quickly and send a perimeter player on the help-side into the lane to prevent or help on the lob pass. The emphasis again is to defend five-against- three. If a team starts to run clear outs, we keep the defender, guarding the man who is clearing out, in the lane for quick help on the baseline. If a team utilizes a 1-4 low, then we move our defenders "up the line" to give early help.

Our man-to-man defense is our bread and butter. We must play great man-to- man. We know that we will play man-to-man every time we don't score. Therefore, we must condition our players to convert quickly and communicate in transition. We must believe that without ever setting a single trap, we can apply unmerciful pressure on the offense and force bad passes and bad shots. We also drill extensively on rebounding every shot that misses. We do not want to give up second shots.

I n many games, a team's best offense is just to get a shot off and attack the boards. Because we are not always in a great rebounding position, we must develop the habit of instinctively fighting for position while the ball is still in the air. We expect all five defenders to reach the "B" area (refer to Diagram 3-3) and block out. Once we are able to rebound, we put immediate pressure on our opponent by running a fast break and scoring in transition.

As illustrated in Diagram 3-3, we divide the court into four specific areas (labeled A, B, C, D) for three reasons:

- To give our players specific shooting-percentage goals on offense.

- To give our players a specific area to rebound.

- To give our players a specific idea as to where and when to trap.

AREAS ON THE COURT

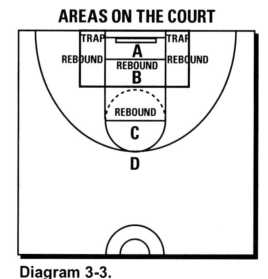

Diagram 3-3.

Being a great man-to-man pressure defensive team requires great dedication. Your players must commit themselves to working relentlessly each and every day in practice. Hard work, a relentless man-to-man pressure, and the Scramble Defense are what separates us from all other teams. As a coach, you cannot expect great changes overnight. After years of practice, we are still improving in this area.

Now that our man-to-man philosophy has been installed, we are ready to start teaching The Scramble.

4

THUMBS DOWN

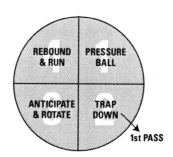

SCRAMBLE THUMBS DOWN

The "Scramble" is the ultimate man-to-man trapping defense currently being played. All five defensive players have man-to-man assignments, but once the first trap is set, each player must be willing to rotate to the open man and be prepared to guard someone else's man.

The Scramble can serve several purposes, including:

- To disrupt the normal rhythm of your opponent.
- To force your opponent out of their offense.
- To force your opponent to prepare differently for you than any other team.
- To create an uptempo game (i.e., 80 to 100 possessions).
- To force a turnover.
- To force a quick shot.
- To force your opponent to make quick decisions.
- To create excitement defensively for your players.
- To create excitement for the fans.
- To force the opponent's point guard to give up the ball.
- To limit a great player.
- To show the offense a different look.
- To offset a team that likes to set screens, or does a lot of cutting.

The Scramble involves two components:

- Thumbs down
- Thumbs up

SCRAMBLE MEANS HUSTLE

Before we begin teaching the half-court Scramble, there are some basic keys to understanding the defensive concepts inherent in The Scramble. Although five defensive men are always on the court, The Scramble only involves three positions.

In The Scramble, you are one of the following:

- *A trapper* – you are in the trap.
- *An interceptor* – You are one of the two players anticipating the pass out of the trap, looking for a steal or deflection. It is important that one of a team's interceptors anticipates the most likely pass out of the trap to the high post. The other interceptor should look for the reversal pass. In other words, make it look open, then take it away.
- *The goaltender* – You are defending the basket area and are looking to take the charge, block the shot, or take away any pass into the low-post.

Four keys make the half-court Scramble work consistently well:

- *Ball pressure* – Constant pressure must be put on the man with the ball.
- *Surprise* – The ball handler should be surprised by our traps.
- *Anticipation* – Everyone must anticipate the next rotation.
- *Hustle* – All five players must be moving and hustling at all times. While there will be times when the defense is going to be out of position, we expect the defenders to make up for it with pure hustle.

THUMBS DOWN

"Thumbs Down" refers to trapping the entry pass receiver and all downward passes. The following rules apply to Thumbs Down:

- Pressure the ball.
- Everyone moves in the direction of the ball.
- Beat the ball to the pass receiver.
- Trappers – seal traps with their hands high, legs crossed, mirroring the ball.
- Interceptors – anticipate the pass, rotate.
- Steal, deflect, or defend any pass out of the trap.
- "Run to where your help came from" when leaving a trap.
- Make a pass look open – then take it away.
- Continue to trap under either of the following conditions: a downward pass; or the player receiving the pass is only 15' to 20' away.
- Recover to man-to-man on ball reversal.
- Contest every shot.
- "Run to rebound"; be prepared to rebound, especially trappers.

* Note: perform all drills to both sides of the floor, so that every player knows the ballside as well as the help-side.

TEACHING THUMBS DOWN STEP-BY-STEP

Step 1   Thumbs Down. 3-on-3—(point, wing #1, wing # 2)—(refer to Diagram 4-1).

O_1 starts with the ball at three-quarters court. He dribbles across mid-court. O_2 and O_3 are the wings ready to receive an entry pass. X_1 pressures the ball. X_2 and X_3 pressure the wings. When the entry pass is made:

(1) X_1 tries to beat the ball to O_2 and set the trap.

(2) X_3 rotates to steal the return pass.

(3) O_2 tries a return pass to O_1.

(4) X_3 steals the pass and team $X_1 X_2 X_3$ converts lay-ups.

(5) Team O becomes defense. Team ABC enters on offense.

Step 2   Thumbs Down. 3-on-3 – with one-man rotation (refer to Diagram 4-2).

Same as Step # 1 but do not steal the reversal pass from O_2 to O_1.

(1) O_2 passes to O_1. X_3 rotates for the steal, but is late. He pressures O_1.

(2) X_1 leaves the trap and "runs to where his help came from." Since X_3 helped take O_1 then X_1 must take O_3. He then pressures O_3.

(3) We are now back to man-to-man coverage.

Question. Why does X_1 run to find the open man?

Answer: Whoever leaves his man to trap down is responsible for finding the open man once the ball is passed out of the trap.

Step 3   Thumbs Down. 4-on-4 – with a two-man rotation (refer to Diagram 4-3).

Set up with a point, two wings, one low-post on the help-side.

(1) X_1 pressures the ball at three-quarters court.

(2) X_2, X_3, and X_4 pressure the wings and low-post.

(3) On the entry pass from O_1 to O_2, X_1 traps with X_2.

(4) X_3 then rotates to O_1.

(5) O_2 passes to O_1. No steal.

(6) O_1 passes to O_3. X_4 anticipates the pass. He can go for the steal or get there a little late and pressure O_3.

(7) X_1 "runs to where his help comes from." He runs toward O_3 until he sees that X_4 is already there. He then sprints to cover O_4.

Step 4   Thumbs Down. 5-on-5. (Refer to Diagram 4-4).

Same as Step # 3 but add another low-post player. 1-2-2 set. Make the entry pass to O_2.

(1) Be certain the ball side low-post is fronted since he is the goaltender.

(2) X_1 and X_2 are trappers.

(3) X_3 and X_4 are interceptors. Be sure X_4 anticipates someone flashing into the high post.

Step 5   Live Action. 4-on-4-on-4.

Play three teams of four. Play a mini-game to five points. The only way to score is on defense.

Rules:

(1) Half a point for a deflection.

(2) One point for a steal.

(3) One point for a basket in conversion.

(4) If the offense scores, offense goes to defense, and a new team comes in on offense.

(5) Offense to defense to off.

(6) If the defense scores in conversion, the new team replaces the offensive team.

Step 6   Thumbs Down/Man-to-Man. 5-on-5 live.

Two teams. The team on defense plays either man-to-man or Thumbs Down. The coach can signal the defense from the sideline. Play a game to five points. All points are scored by the defense.

Rules:

(1) Half a point for a deflection.

(2) One point for a steal.

(3) One point for a defensive rebound.

(4) One point for a basket in conversion.

(5) If the offensive team scores, convert from offense to defense and continue the drill.

DIAGRAM 4-1. THUMBS DOWN – 3-ON-3

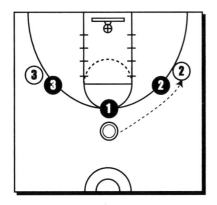

- O1 passes the ball to O2
- X1 tries to beat the ball to O2

Diagram 4-1a.

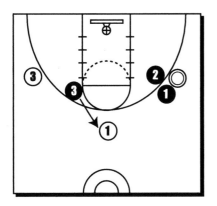

- X1 and X2 trap O2

Diagram 4-1b.

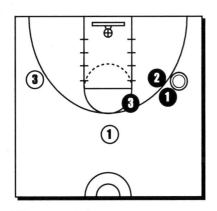

- O2 tries to return pass to O1
- X3 rotates and steals pass
- X3 breaks for a lay-up or dunk

Diagram 4-1c.

DIAGRAM 4-2. THUMBS DOWN – 3-ON-3, WITH ONE -MAN ROTATION

Diagram 4-2a.

- O2 passes the ball to O1

- X3 does not get steal, he pressures O1

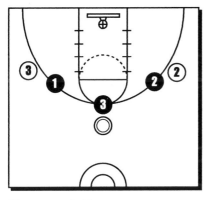

Diagram 4-2b.

- X1, X2, X3 are back playing man-to-man

DIAGRAM 4-3. THUMBS DOWN – 4-ON-4, WITH TWO -MAN ROTATION

Diagram 4-3a.

- X1 pressures the ball

- X1, X3, and X4 pressure the wings and the low post

DIAGRAM 4-3. THUMBS DOWN – 4-ON-4, WITH TWO -MAN ROTATION (CONTINUED)

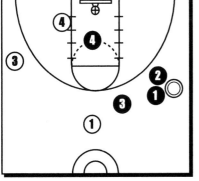

Diagram 4-3b.

- On entry pass from 01 to 02, X1 and X2 trap 02

- X3 rotates, anticipating a return pass from 02 to 01

- X4 moves in the direction of the pass

Diagram 4-3c.

- 02 passes the ball to 01

- X3 does not get steal; he pressures 01

- X1 "runs" out of the trap, looking for where his help came from

- X4 rotates, anticipating next pass from 01 to 03

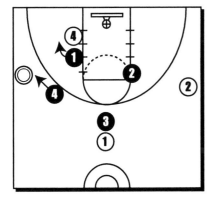

Diagram 4-3d.

- 01 passes the ball to 03

- X4 can go for steal or get out to pressure 03

- X1 sees X4 going out to 03; he then sprints down to cover 04

- X2 moves in the direction of the pass

DIAGRAM 4-3. THUMBS DOWN – 4-ON-4, WITH TWO -MAN ROTATION (CONTINUED)

Diagram 4-3e.

- X1, X2, X3 and X4 are now back playing man-to-man

- X1 must work hard to front 04 in the post

DIAGRAM 4-4. THUMBS DOWN – 5-ON-5

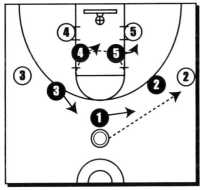

Diagram 4-4a.

- X1 pressures the ball

- X2, X3, X4 and X5 pressure the wings and the posts

Diagram 4-4b.

- On the entry pass from 01 to 02, X1 and X2 trap 02

- X3 rotates, anticipating a return pass from 02 to 01

- X5 must front the ballside low post

- X4 rotates up and covers the high post

DIAGRAM 4-4. THUMBS DOWN – 5-ON-5 (CONTINUED)

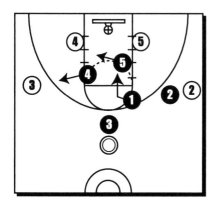

Diagram 4-4c.

- O2 passes the ball to O1

- X3 does not get steal; he then pressures O1

- X1 "runs" out of the trap

- X4 rotates, anticipating the next pass from O1 to O3

- X5 gets back inside O5; he serves as the goaltender

Diagram 4-4d.

- O1 passes the ball to O3

- X4 can go for steal or get out to pressure O3

- X5 rotates over to cover O4

- X1 sees X4 going out to O3 and X5 going over to O4

- X2 moves in the direction of the pass

Diagram 4-4e.

- X5 must work hard to front O4 in the post

- X1 drops down to cover O5

- X2, X3, and X4 are now back playing man-to-man

What happens if the ball is passed to the corner? The answer is simple, it is an automatic trap. We like to encourage teams to pass the ball to the corner. We believe that the corner is a terrible place for the offense to have the ball, because it eliminates so many passing options. If the offensive team passes the ball to the corner, then the defender (X_2) whose man passed the ball to the corner, should leave him and trap down. When the ball is passed out of the trap, (X_2) is then responsible for leaving the trap and defending the open man. The following steps are involved in trapping in the corner:

- 0_1 passes to 0_2.

- X_1 traps with X_2.

- 0_2 passes to the corner to 0_4.

- X_2 leaves his man and traps the corner pass with X_4.

- When 0_2 passes it out of the trap, X_2 must leave the trap and find the open man.

Thumbs Down is the most conservative component of The Scramble. You simply trap down on the first pass and rotate back to a man-to-man after one ball reversal. Thumbs Down is also the safest form of The Scramble. Safest, because after one trap, you are back to man-to-man coverage and are not gambling beyond the first pass. However, to make The Scramble truly effective, we also like to trap down on any pass to the corner.

We believe the weakest skill of players today is passing – a limitation that is especially true of front-court players. That is why we are convinced that The Scramble is so effective. So few players have the ability to spot the open man, the skill to make the pass, and the poise to make it under the pressure of being double teamed.

Thumbs Down is an excellent half-court pressure defense. It allows you to trap the opponent's first pass receiver and immediately take your opponent out of their normal half-court offense. Since the likely pass out of the trap is a return pass to the point guard who is standing still and wide open, this pass is an easy one to anticipate and steal by the wing defender opposite the ball. If he does steal it, he almost always ends up with a breakaway lay-up. When this occurs, two additional things typically happen: your defense gets pumped up, and your pressure defense improves; and the offensive team becomes cautious and more tentative.

Because no player wants to be trapped, the offense often starts going away from the basket to avoid the trap. Even if the wing defender is a little late and can't make the steal, he will still be there in time to pressure the point guard and allow his teammates to rotate back into man-to-man. As a result, you have given your team an excellent chance to force a turnover; you have taken the other team out of their offense, and you haven't lost anything.

If you are going to choose just one Scramble defense, I recommend Thumbs Down. Your rotation should be 15 to 20 feet, and the nearest defender should pick up the open man. When leaving the trap, your defensive man that is rotating should not look to see if the pass out of the trap was stolen. This is a common mistake. The point guard leaving the first trap must instinctively move quickly to "run to where his help came from." Any hesitation will cause him to be late in his rotation. The quicker your point guard is in getting to the trap and then leaving the trap after the pass out of the trap, the better the defense. Our point guard is drilled daily on trapping and rotating. He must realize the importance of his role and take that job very seriously. Keep in mind that if your point guard is weak, then your defense is weak. There is no doubt about that. On the other hand, if your point guard is a relentless worker with good speed and quickness, you can use Thumbs Down effectively, even if no one else on your team is particularly quick.

We sometimes take our fastest player, even if he is not our point guard, and put him on the dribbler. Giving someone this important role often increases his confidence and gives him an identity that he wouldn't otherwise have on offense.

When Antonio Daniels was our point guard at Bowling Green, he was always assigned a wing player to defend. We then moved Demar Moore, a very fast 2 guard to defend at the point. These assignments gave us two distinct advantages. First, Daniels did not have to tire himself out by pressuring the ball handler full-court the entire game. He was our offensive quarterback and could concentrate his efforts in this area. Secondly, Moore was a role player on offense. He could put all of his energy into pressuring the ball. He soon developed a reputation for being a great defender. He led the Mid-American Conference in steals and was named defensive player-of-the-year. His self-esteem grew throughout the season as his teammates, coaches, and the media gave him credit for forcing so many turnovers.

The same was true in 1984 when Ricky Stokes, now the head men's basketball coach at Virginia Tech, won the national player-of-the-year award for players under six feet tall. Stokes was not known for his offense but for his tremendous defense. He was able to carve out a role that earned him national recognition. In a similar vein, our back-up point guard at George Mason, Tremaine Price, has been affectionately nicknamed "The Junk Yard Dog" for this spark-plug role as a defensive specialist coming in off the bench. These players were not the primary offensive point guards. They were given specific jobs and they created images that everyone loved. In the process, they became fan favorites.

Tremaine Price said, "I have to face The Scramble everyday in practice. It drives me crazy. It's like there are six defenders on the court at one time. There always seems to be two men on me, and no one else is open. I know how it feels, so when I come in the game I am anxious to put that kind of pressure on our opponent, and it all starts with our man-to-man". The point to keep in mind is that developing a defensive reputation can really add to a player's level of self-esteem.

Look at your personnel and evaluate them carefully. Who is your best on-the-ball defender? Can he pressure the ball? If the answer to whether your best on-the-ball defender can pressure the ball is yes, then you can be an excellent Thumbs Down team.

5

THUMBS UP

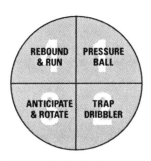

SCRAMBLE THUMBS UP

"Thumbs Up" refers to trapping the dribbler. The following rules apply to Thumbs Up:

- Pressure the ball.

- Surprise the dribbler, trap up.

- Anticipate and rotate.

- Seal the trap. Hands high. Legs crossed. Mirror the ball.

- Steal, deflect, or defend any pass out of the trap.

- "Run to where your help came from" when leaving a trap.

- Make a pass look open, then take it away.

- Continue to trap on downward pass when either of the following conditions exist: a down ward pass, not outward; or the player receiving the pass is 15' to 20' feet away.

- Trap the dribbler on all ball screens.

- Know your job – trapper, interceptor, or goaltender.

Note: perform all drills to both sides of the floor, so every player knows his role.

WHY AND WHEN TO USE THUMBS UP?

Thumbs Up is the most aggressive component of the half-court Scramble. Rather than wait for another team to initiate their offense, we elect to trap the dribbler as soon as the ball crosses mid-court or is dribbled to the wing. Thumbs Up is especially effective in the following four situations:

- To get the ball out of the hands of an excellent ball handler by trapping him at mid-court.

- To attack the point guard, if the point guard is a little shaky and we feel that he can be rattled with a quick trap.

- To create a scramble situation when an opponent is not making an entry pass but is using a dribble entry to begin their offense.

- To keep a great player from catching the first pass. We do not want the point guard to pass the ball to the best player, allowing him to be the decision maker. We double the point guard and rotate to the wing to keep the best player from catching the ball.

Note: It is important to teach your players that Thumbs Up will become Thumbs Down after the initial trap up on the dribbler.

TEACHING THUMBS UP STEP-BY-STEP:

Step 1   "Thumbs Up". 3-on-3 (a point, a wing, a low post ballside).
(Refer to Diagram 5-1).

0_1 begins with the ball at three-quarters court. X_1 pressures him to the side. X_2 leaves 0_2 as the ball crosses the mid-court line sealing a trap at half-court with X_1.

(1) X_1 and X_2 trap 0_1.

(2) X_3 anticipates the pass to 0_2.

(3) When 0_1 passes to 0_2, X_3 tries to steal it.

(4) If X_3 is a little late, he pressures the ball.

(5) X_1 traps down with X_3 on a pass from 0_1 to 0_2.

(6) X2 will become an interceptor.

Note: Thumbs Up becomes Thumbs Down on any entry pass. At that point, Thumbs Down rules apply.

Step 2   Thumbs Up. 4-on-4 (a point, two wings, one low post). (Refer to Diagram 5-2).

(1) O_1 can dribble to either side.

(2) X_2 leaves his man to trap the dribble.

(3) X_3 and X_4 anticipate the pass and get ready to rotate.

(4) If O_1 passes to O_2 X_1 and X_4 trap O_2.

(5) X_3 becomes the goaltender. X_2 is an interceptor.

Note: In Step # 2, the offense must cooperate. The offense should not be trying to score. You should remember to initiate offense on both sides of the floor.

Step 3   Thumbs Up. 5-on-5 (a point, two wings, two low-posts). (Refer to Diagram 5-3).

(1) O_1 can dribble to either side.

(2) X_1 pressures the ball.

(3) If O_1 dribbles toward O_2, then X_2 comes up to trap at mid-court.

(4) X_4 anticipates the pass to O_2.

(5) X_5 helps X_4. X_3 also helps and is ready to rotate.

(6) If O_1 passes to O_2, X_1 and X_4 trap. X_2 and X_3 are interceptors. X_5, the goaltender, fronts the the low post.

Step 4   Live 5-on-5. Thumbs Up/Thumbs Down/man-to-man.

Two teams. The team on defense plays either man-to-man, Thumbs Down, or Thumbs Up. The coach signals the defense from the sideline. The game is played to five points. All points are scored by the defense.

Rules:

(1) Half a point for a deflection.

(2) One point for a steal.

(3) One point for a defensive rebound.

(4) One point for a basket in conversion.

(5) If the offensive team scores, the two teams switch their roles and continue the drill.

DIAGRAM 5-1. THUMBS UP– 3-ON-3

Diagram 5-1a.

- X1 pressures the ball handler to the sideline

- X2 and X3 are "up the line," off their men

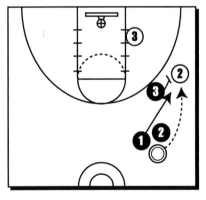

Diagram 5-1b.

- X2 leaves O2 as the ball crosses mid-court

- X1 and X2 trap O1

- X3 rotates up, anticipating a pass from to O2

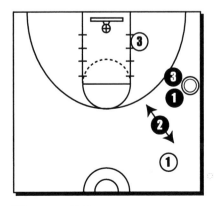

Diagram 5-1c.

- X3 does not get the steal, so he pressures O2

- X1 "runs" out of the trap following the downward pass

- X1 and X3 trap O2

- X2 drops off O1 to be in a help position

DIAGRAM 5-2. THUMBS UP— 4-ON-4

- X1 pressures the ball handler to the sideline

- X2, X3, and X4 are "up the line," off their men

Diagram 5-2a.

- X2 leaves O2 as the ball crosses mid-court

- X1 and X2 trap O1

- X4 rotates up, anticipating a pass from O1 to O2

- X3 rotates to the middle as the trap occurs away from him

Diagram 5-2b.

- If X4 does not get the steal, he pressures O2

- X1 "runs" out of the trap following the downward pass

- X1 and X4 trap O2

- X3 (the goaltender) rotates to cover O4

- X2 drops off O1 to be in a help position

Diagram 5-2c.

DIAGRAM 5-3. THUMBS UP— 5-ON-5

Diagram 5-3a.

- X1 pressures the ball handler to the sideline

- X2, X3, X4, and X5 are "up the line," off their men

Diagram 5-3b.

- X2 leaves O2 as the ball crosses midcourt

- X1 and X2 trap O1

- X4 rotates up, anticipating a pass from O1 to O2

- X5 (the goaltender) rotates over to cover O4

- X3 rotates to the middle as the trap occurs away from him

Diagram 5-3c.

- If X4 does not get the steal, he pressures O2

- X1 "runs" out of the trap following the downward pass

- X1 and X4 trap O2

- X5 fronts the low post

- X3 plays the high-post area

- X2 drops off O1 to be in help position

In 1989 and then again in 1990, my Bowling Green team faced the Big-10 Champions, Michigan State, who were led by their All-American point guard 6'8", Steve Smith. We knew before the game that we could not allow Smith to control the game. Throughout his career, Smith had dominated the opposition. We decided to utilize The Scramble at the three-quarter-court level regularly throughout the game. Thumbs Up was our best option. This way we would trap Smith and force the other players to make big plays. The strategy worked. Bowling Green became the first visiting team to win at Michigan State in its new state-of-the-art Breslin Center. A shocked, sell-out crowd of 15,000 fans left the arena stunned when we pulled out the 80-79 victory.

The Spartans returned to Bowling Green the next season, undefeated and ranked fifth in the nation, looking for revenge. Instead of demolishing us, like most of the experts predicted, we forced 22 turnovers and cruised to a 98-85 victory. Thumbs Up had done it again. Smith played his typical great game; but when he was trapped, and forced to give it up, he never got it back.

We were now developing the reputation as a "giant killer." After beating Kentucky at Rupp Arena in 1988, and defeating Michigan State back to back in 1989 and 90, people were beginning to take notice. The Scramble Defense was slowly becoming our trademark. During the 90's, we continued to upset highly regarded teams by knocking off Big-Ten foes Ohio State, Penn State and Purdue.

"I love The Scramble," says George Evans, a John Wooden Award nominee for 1999-2000. "I love seeing the facial reactions of the other team's point guard when he is being trapped. You can see 'panic' in his face. No one likes being trapped, no matter how good you are."

6

FULL-COURT SCRAMBLE

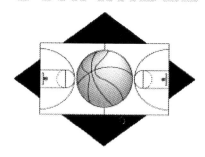

One of the best ways to demoralize your opponent, and fire up your own team in the process, is to jump on your opponent from the opening tip. A quick start is always a good sign, whether you are the home team or the visiting team. Nothing gets your home crowd going and into a game better than a tremendous explosion of intensity following the opening tip. To start the game, we like to get a quick score and be in the full-court Scramble immediately. We like to apply a knock-out punch, before our opponent knows what hit him. We want to create the action and be the aggressor for the full 40 minutes.

By the same token, when we are on the road we like to take the crowd out of the game as soon as possible. We also want to send a message to the officials that we are going "to get after it" from start to finish. We believe that we can earn the respect of the officials by how hard we play. Even if we get a few fouls called on us early, we believe that all factors considered, we end up with an advantage by the time the opponent adjusts to our pressure.

"55"

"55" is the component of the full-court Scramble that allows us to put the greatest pressure on our opponent as quickly as possible. Because "55" begins as a zone press, each defensive player can move instinctively to his defensive position after a score. We want our players to sprint to their spots and then find a man to match up with in their area. "55" also allows us to develop a good "4" man. The 4 man is always "on the ball" in "55". We want him to be very active. We want him to make the inbounds pass as difficult as possible. The bigger he is, the better. We want our 4 man to take away any pass toward the middle of the court. We want our opponent to make the inbounds pass to someone up the sideline. The 4 man then becomes a trapper as soon as the inbounds pass is completed. The 4 man and the ball side wing (3 or 2) then trap the ball handler. The opposite wing (3 or 2) and our point guard (1) then become interceptors and anticipate any pass out of the trap. The 5 man goes deep and becomes the goaltender. Once the ball is passed out of the trap, we look for the steal or convert quickly to half-court defense.

QUICK TRAP/SLOW TRAP/TWIST

After a short while, we change our defense after scores from "55" to either quick trap, slow trap, or twist. We now match up man-to-man and look to deny the inbounds pass with more individual responsibility. We continue to trap the first pass, look for the steal, and then convert quickly if the offense goes through the press. It is mandatory that your players communicate in conversion. It is not enough for a defender to call out his man. He must do it three times to let everyone know "who has who." This step also tends to intimidate the offensive player who now knows the defense has everyone covered.

FULL-COURT SCRAMBLE

The following rules apply to the full-court Scramble:

- Convert quickly from offense to defense.
- Deny the inbounds pass.
- Apply all rules from Thumbs Down and Thumbs Up.
- Develop good habits for each player.
- Someone must call "ball" in conversion.

COMPONENTS OF THE FULL-COURT SCRAMBLE

The full-court Scramble has five components:

- Man-to-man.
- Quick trap.
- Slow trap.
- Twist.
- "55".

The following rules apply to each of the various components of the full-court Scramble:

MAN-TO-MAN: (Refer to Diagram 6-1).

- Convert quickly from offense to defense.
- Deny the inbounds pass; ball-you-man defense; look for a deflection.
- Fake the trap on all dribblers (open/close/open/close).
- The man defending the dribbler must "turn him" three times by half-court.

DIAGRAM 6-1. FULL-COURT MAN-TO-MAN

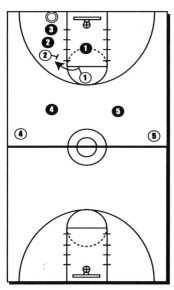

- X3 pressures the inbounds pass

- X1 and X2 deny the inbounds pass, looking for deflections

- X4 and X5 guard their men and protect against the long pass

Diagram 6-1a.

- O2 screens for O1

- X2 and X1 switch on the screen and deny the inbounds pass

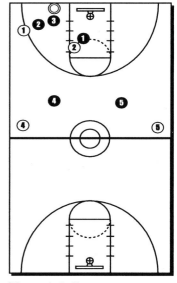

Diagram 6-1b.

- O3 inbounds to O1

- X1, X2, and X3 must fake the trap on all dribblers

- X2 must "turn" O1 three times by half court

- X4 and X5 guard their men as they move into the front court

Diagram 6-1c.

QUICK TRAP: (Refer to Diagram 6-2).

- Convert quickly; pick up your own man.
- Put great pressure on the inbound passer.
- Deny the inbounds pass; look for a deflection, but do not gamble.
- When pass is completed, trap the pass receiver.
- One trap and out – convert quickly to half-court man.
- Another option: two traps and out – convert quickly (coaches option).
- Pursuit – if the ball goes over your head, chase it from behind.
- Know who you are (i.e., trapper; interceptor; goaltender).
- Anticipate and rotate – man in trap – find the open man. "Run to where your help comes from."
- Communicate – call out your man three times as you convert.
- Recover to half-court man-to-man.

Note: Someone must call "ball" in conversion.

SLOW TRAP: (Refer to Diagram 6-3).

- Convert quickly from offense to defense (man-to-man).
- Pressure the inbounds pass but do not gamble.
- Do not trap the pass receiver immediately.
- Force the dribbler to the middle; do not get beat sideline.
- Trap the ball handler on his first dribble.
- If the ball handler continues to dribble, herd him; force him to pick up the ball.
- One trap and out.
- Know who you are (i.e., trapper; interceptor; goaltender).
- Anticipate and rotate.
- Pursuit – if the ball goes over your head, chase it from behind.
- Communicate – call out your man three times as you convert.
- Recover to half-court, man-to-man.

Note: Someone must call "ball" in conversion.

DIAGRAM 6-2. FULL-COURT QUICK TRAP

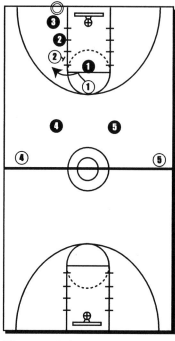

- X3 pressures the inbounds pass

- X1 and X2 deny the inbounds pass, looking for deflections

- X4 and X5 guard their men and protect against the long pass

Diagram 6-2a.

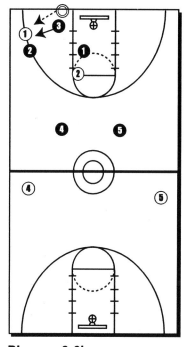

- O2 screens for O1

- X2 and X1 switch on the screen and deny the inbounds pass

Diagram 6-2b.

DIAGRAM 6-2. FULL-COURT QUICK TRAP (CONTINUED)

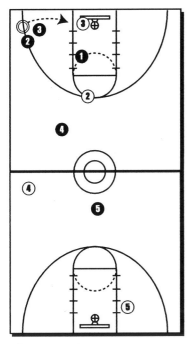

- O3 inbounds to O1

- X3 and X2 trap O1

- X1 "splits" O3 and O2, looking to intercept an errant pass

- X4 "splits" O2 and O4, looking to intercept an errant pass

- X5 drops back and acts as the goaltender

Diagram 6-2c.

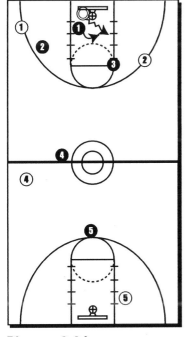

- O1 passes the ball back to O3

- X1 moves up and pressures O3

- X3 "runs" out of the trap to where his help came from and guards O2

- X2 guards O1

- X4 drops back and guards O4

- X5 drops back and guards O5

Diagram 6-2d.

DIAGRAM 6-3. FULL-COURT SLOW TRAP

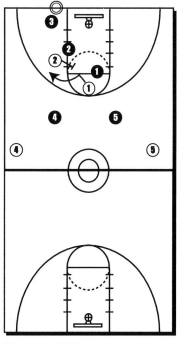

- X3 pressures the inbounds pass

- X1 and X2 deny the inbounds pass, looking for deflections

- X4 and X5 guard their men and protect against the long pass

Diagram 6-3a.

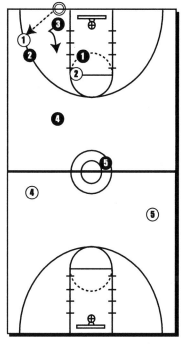

- O2 screens for O1

- X2 and X1 switch on the screen and deny the inbounds pass

Diagram 6-3b.

DIAGRAM 6-3. FULL-COURT SLOW TRAP (CONTINUED)

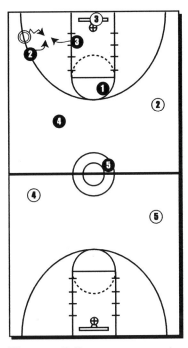

Diagram 6-3c.

- O3 inbounds to O1

- X2 pressures O1, forcing him to the middle

- X3 guards O3, anticipating that O1 will start dribbling

- X1 and X4 guard their men, anticipating becoming interceptors

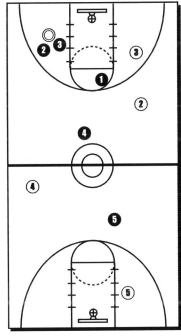

Diagram 6-3d.

- O1 takes one dribble to the middle

- X3 and X2 trap O1

- X1 "splits" O3 and O2, looking to intercept an errant pass

- X4 "splits" O2 and O4, looking to intercept an errant pass

- X5 drops back and acts as the goaltender

TWIST: (Refer to Diagram 6-4).

- Convert quickly from offense to defense (man-to-man).
- The defender on the ball turns his back on the ball and denies the most likely receiver.
- If the pass is completed, he traps immediately.
- You may want to deny the point guard or best free-throw shooter.
- Deny inbounds pass. Look for a five-second violation.
- One trap and out.
- Convert quickly to half-court man-to-man.
- Pursuit – if ball goes over your head, chase it from behind.
- Communicate – call out your man three times.

Note: Someone must call "ball" in conversion.

"55": (1-2-1-1 MATCH-UP ZONE PRESS) (Refer to Diagram 6-5).

- Convert quickly from offense to defense to a specific "area."
- 4 is on the ball. He is always in the first trap. 3 is to 4's left. 3 is either a trapper or an interceptor. 2 is to 4's right. 2 is either a trapper or an interceptor. 1 is in the middle. 1 is always an interceptor. 5 is back. 5 is always the goaltender.
- Match up as quickly as possible while ball is out of bounds.
- Deny inbounds.
- Trap the first pass; one trap and out; 4 will trap with either 2 or 3.
- Anticipate and rotate.
- Pursuit – if the ball goes over your head, chase it from behind.
- Communicate in conversion, call out your man three times.
- Recover man-to-man.

Note: Someone must call "ball" in conversion.

DIAGRAM 6-4. FULL-COURT TWIST

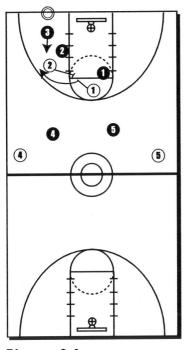

- X3 turns his back to O3 and helps deny the most likely pass receive

- X1 and X2 deny the inbounds pass, looking for deflections

- X4 and X5 guard their men, protecting against the long pass

Diagram 6-4a.

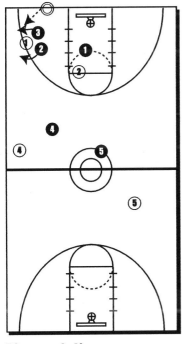

- O2 screens for O1

- X2 and X1 switch on the screen and deny the inbounds pass

- X3 picks up O1 coming off the screen and denies the inbounds pass

Diagram 6-4b.

DIAGRAM 6-4. FULL-COURT TWIST (CONTINUED)

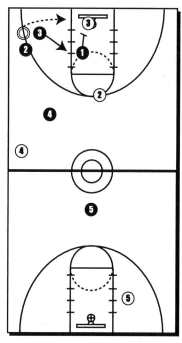

- O3 inbounds to O1

- X3 and X2 trap O1

- X1 "splits" O3 and O2, looking to intercept an errant pass

- X4 "splits" O2 and O4, looking to intercept an errant pass

- X5 drops back and acts as the goaltender

Diagram 6-4c.

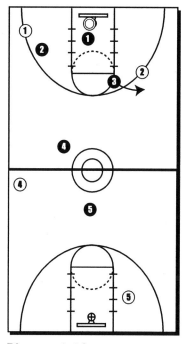

- O1 passes the ball back to O3

- X1 moves up and pressures O3

- X3 "runs" out of the trap to where his help came from and guards O2

- X2 guards O1

- X4 drops back and guards O4

- X5 drops back and guards O5

Diagram 6-4d.

DIAGRAM 6-5. FULL-COURT "55"

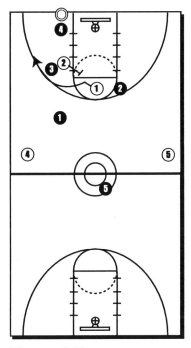

- · X4 is on the ball, pressuring the inbounds pass

- · X3 is on X4's left, denying the inbounds pass to O2

- · X2 is on X4's right, denying the inbounds pass to O1

- · X1 is in the middle, able to get to a pass to O4

- · X5, as the goaltender, protects against the long pass

Diagram 6-5a.

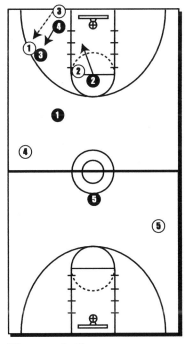

- · O2 screens for O1

- · X3 plays his area, denying the inbounds pass to O1

- · X2 plays his area, denying the inbounds pass to O2

- · X1 plays the middle, looking for cutters and anyone who might be able to get to a pass to O4

- · X5 is the goaltender

Diagram 6-5b.

DIAGRAM 6-5. FULL-COURT "55" (CONTINUED)

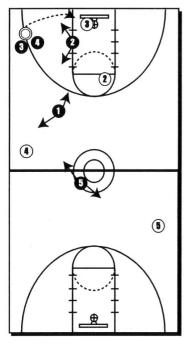

Diagram 6-5c.

- O3 inbounds to O1

- X4 and X3 trap O1

- X2 aggressively moves forward, anticipating the pass back to O3

- X1 plays the middle and anticipates the pass to the middle or the sideline

- X5 is the goaltender

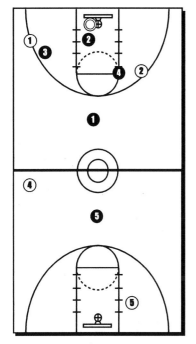

Diagram 6-5d.

- O1 passes the ball back to O3

- If X2 does not get the steal, he guards O3

- X4 "runs" out of the trap to where his help came from and guards O2

- X1 drops back and guards the middle

- X5 is the goaltender

Note: X1 may move forward to pick up O2. In this case, O4 would continue to "run" to where his help came from and drop back to the middle, eventually picking up O4 in the front court.

The full-court Scramble is most effective when employed to start the game, start the second half, and end the game. It is important to spend a great deal of time working on your conversion from offense to your full-court press. We want our players to develop the habit of scoring and pressing. We want to be the aggressor. We spend a lot of time working our half-court offense into our press in order to develop our players' instincts for full-court pressure defense.

"The full-court Scramble is the best," says Jay Larranaga, now a professional basketball player in France. Larranaga was an outstanding defensive player in The Scramble during his four years at Bowling Green. "I thought it would be difficult for everyone to learn The Scramble. However, after playing the full- court Scramble each and every day at practice for weeks, everyone knew what to do. The drills really helped develop good habits and confidence in what we were trying to do. Once everybody knew their job, it was easy and lots of fun."

7

SCRAMBLE DRILLS

We like to use a very simple teaching method with all our drills. We believe that players learn best by watching, then by doing. It has been said on numerous occasions that, "imitation is the greatest form of flattery." We believe imitation is also the key to learning. The five simple steps that we employ to teach each drill are:

- Explanation

- Demonstration

- Imitation

- Correction

- Repetition

After a brief explanation from the coach, we have our veteran players show our inexperienced players how to do a drill properly. By asking your older players to demonstrate a skill, you create a leadership role for them that can help them build confidence and pride in what you want them to do. Once an experienced player demonstrates the proper technique, we expect the other players to imitate it. If their imitation is not what we expect, we make corrections. The point to be emphasized in this instance is that we do not criticize, we instruct.

FOOD FOR THOUGHT

I'd rather see a lesson than to hear one any day,

I'd rather you'd walk with me than to merely show the way.

The eye's a better teacher and more willing than the ear,

And counsel is confusing but examples always clear.

The best of all the teachers are the ones who live the creed,

To see good put in action is what everybody needs.

I soon can learn to do it if you let me see it done,

I can see your hand in action but your tongue too fast may run.

And the counsel you are giving may be very fine and true,

But I'd rather get my lesson by observing what you do!

— Author Unknown

We believe that every player wants to execute the plays correctly. Accordingly, you should "teach" those who are making mistakes, not criticize them.

In his book, *Lend Me Your Ears,* William Safire states, "Great teachers don't teach. They help students learn. Students teach themselves. Two of the all-time greats – Socrates and Jesus Christ – spoke briefly, painting pictures and telling tales (parables), and always raised more questions than they settled. The greatest teacher makes a few simple points. The powerful teacher leaves one or two fundamental truths. And the memorable teacher makes the point by not *telling,* but by helping the students *discover* on their own. Learning takes place through discovery, not when you're told something but when you figure it out for yourself. All a really fine teacher does is make suggestions, point out the problems, and above all, ask questions, and more questions, and more questions."

We agree with Mr. Safire. That is why we teach through explanation, demonstration, imitation, correction, and constant repetition. Once everyone knows the drill, then we will repeat it often to develop good habits. A skilled player does not think through each step of a particular drill. He executes on the basis of his instincts.

LAW OF INERTIA

We like to ask our players during a practice a simple question, "What is the Law of Inertia?" At first, no player seems to know the answer or is too embarrassed to say. We explain that the "Law of Inertia" is very important to understanding individual and team defense. The "Law of Inertia" states that a body in motion tends to stay in motion, and a body at rest tends to stay at rest. Since our defensive pressure requires everyone to be moving at all times, we emphasize that our players should keep moving. Don't come to a stand still. Keep your feet moving.

We remind our players constantly throughout practice, and especially in drills, to keep moving their feet even when it doesn't seem to make any sense. During drills, we tell them to bounce, to have "happy feet" (i.e., "dancing feet") to emphasize the importance of constantly having their feet moving. If a player stops, it will take him longer to get started again. This factor is especially a problem in The Scramble because you are either moving to seal a trap, rotating to the next open man, or guarding the basket to prevent a pass or shot. Everyone must move together.

When The Scramble is being executed perfectly, all five men are moving at the same time in the direction of the ball. If a coach shows videotape to his team, everyone can see the players moving together. When you begin teaching The Scramble, the first thing you notice is that the defenders are moving one at a time, like they are in sequence. First, the trapper X1 leaves his man to go trap. Second, X3 rotates to take his man. Then, finally, the goaltender moves to front the low post. This situation (i.e., the sequential moving) must be corrected.

Sometimes to make a teaching point, we have each defender hold a long rope to connect him to the next defender. X1 is connected by a rope in each hand to X2; in turn, X3. X4 and X5 are also connected by a rope. We then execute a 5-on-5 Scramble drill and allow our players to pull each other into the proper position with everyone moving "together."

We have sold our players on defense because we believe great defensive teams win championships. However, the greatest motivation for our players may very well come from one of our other motivational expressions. We constantly emphasize that "our best offense is our pressure defense."

We believe players are highly motivated to score. Everyone wants to put the ball in the basket. When our players realize that a steal converts quickly into a fast-break lay-up, they are more inclined to keep pressure on the ball. They like getting numerous opportunities to score in the open court on lay-ups or dunks. In fact, over the last several seasons, while using The Scramble exclusively, our field-goal percentage and scoring average have increased dramatically.

During the 1996-97 season, for example, our Bowling Green team led the Mid-American Conference in scoring, averaging over 80 points per game. We were also in the Top 20 in the nation in field-goal percentage offense shooting 50 percent from the field. Antonio Daniels, our outstanding point guard (the 1997 MAC Player of the Year, the fourth player chosen in the 1997 NBA Draft, and currently with the San Antonio Spurs) averaged 24 points per game (fifth in the nation) and shot 54 percent from the field. His improvement in scoring – from 16 ppg as a junior to 24 ppg as a senior – and field-goal percentage – from 48 percent to 54 percent – was a direct result of getting several additional dunks each game off of steals. Nothing can give a team or a player more confidence quickly than an easy basket.

At George Mason during the 1998-99 season, we led our league in scoring and field-goal percentage with only one player who was a true inside threat, and no starter over 6'6". Our big man was George Evans, the 1999 CAA Player of the Year, a 6'6, 230 pound, cat-quick post player. Evans led our league, the CAA, in scoring and field-goal percentage. He was also second in steals, and third in rebounding. No doubt exists that Evans and Daniels were able to dominate those statistical categories because of the Scramble Defense. Their ability to anticipate our opponents' passes under pressure and convert steals into lay-ups was a huge factor in producing impressive numbers.

Your players will love to Scramble. They too will be sold on pressure defense when they see the opportunities it creates on offense. They will believe, as we do, that "your best offense is your pressure defense." To perfect The Scramble, we break down the skills to a series of simple drills, such as the following:

DRILL #1. NOSE ON THE BALL. 1-ON-1 (Four steps). (Refer to Diagrams 7-1 and 7-2).

Step 1. One dribble – pinch (dead).

Step 2. Three dribbles – pinch (dead).

Step 3. Zig-zag dribble to mid-court – pinch, pass to coach, deny.

Step 4. Zig-zag – take the charge at mid-court; the dribbler sprints to defense.

DRILL #2. HERDING. 2-ON-1 (two defenders, one offensive player).
(Refer to Diagrams 7-3 to 7-6).

Step 1. Explosive dribble in one direction; pick up the dribble; pinch; practice the trap; hands high; legs crossed.

Step 2. Zig-zag dribble – keep dribbling for five seconds; defenders try to seal the trap – their hands held high and their legs crossed; do not reach; do not foul.

Step 3. Zig-zag plus coach – same as Zig-zag, but when the dribbler is trapped, he passes it out of the trap to a coach; the trappers should sprint back trying to prevent the coach from shooting a lay-up.

Step 4. Herding – 3-on-2, plus coach or 3-on-3 live; add an offensive and defensive player at mid-court. Match-up 3-on-3, with the coach as one offensive player; defense works on slow trap, trapping the dribbler, rotating and converting.

DRILL #3. ANTICIPATION DRILL. (Three steps). (Refer to Diagrams 7-7 and 7-8).

Step 1. Two offensive players O1 and O2 are positioned at each elbow. Coach (c) has the ball 15' to 20' away. Defense X1 splits the two offensive players. Coach attempts to pass to either O1 or O2. X1 must deflect or steal each pass. Each pass is caught and returned to the coach.

Step 2. Anticipation "55" – defend for two passes. Five defensive players (X1 X2 X3 X4 X5) are set up in a 1-2-2 full-court zone press. The coach (c) takes the ball out-of-bounds and attempts to make an inbounds pass to one of his four receivers, O1 O2 O3 O4. The defenders should look to deflect or steal the inbounds pass. If the pass is complete to a wing, then we trap and anticipate the next pass.

Step 3. Free throw/conversion/55 – game to five points. We line up with Team X shooting a free-throw, under game conditions. Team O inbounds after made free-throw. Team X converts to "55" and presses full-court. Play one possession at a time and keep score. Team O then shoots a free-throw and presses.

Scoring rules:
- Any deflection is 1 point.
- Any steal is 1 point.
- Any basket is 1 point.
- Any offensive rebound is 1 point.
- Game to five points; losers run a series of 10-second sprints.

DIAGRAM 7-1. NOSE ON THE BALL – PINCH AT HALF COURT

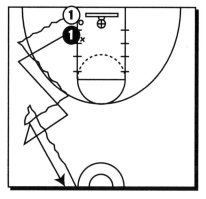

- O1 starts with the ball on the baseline

- X1 guards O1 in a good, low defensive stance

Diagram 7-1a.

DIAGRAM 7-1. NOSE ON THE BALL – PINCH AT HALF COURT (CONTINUED)

Diagram 7-1b.

- O1 takes three dribbles to his right

- X1 guards O1, staying down in a defensive stance

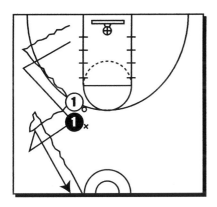

Diagram 7-1c.

- O1 makes a move taking three dribbles to his left

- X1 continues to guard O1, staying down in his defensive stance

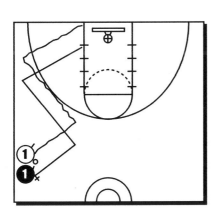

Diagram 7-1d.

- O1 makes a move, takes three dribbles right, and picks the ball up

- X1 guards O1, and calls "pinch" on the dribble pick up

- O1 moves the ball for a few seconds

- X1 shadows the ball

- O1 passes to the coach in the middle of the court

- X1 moves in the direction of the pass into a deny position

DIAGRAM 7-1. NOSE ON THE BALL – PINCH AT HALF COURT (CONTINUED)

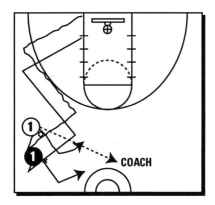

Diagram 7-1e.

- X1 denies the pass back to O1

- O1 moves to get open, and receives the pass back from coach

- "Nose on the ball" continues to the other baseline

DIAGRAM 7-2. NOSE ON THE BALL – TAKE CHARGE AT HALF COURT

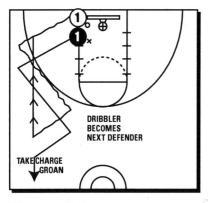

Diagram 7-2a.

- O1 starts with the ball on the baseline

- X1 guards O1 in a good, low defensive stance

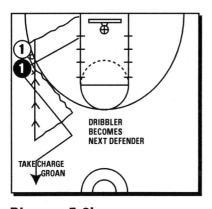

Diagram 7-2b.

- O1 takes three dribbles to his right

- X1 guards O1, staying down in a defensive stance

DIAGRAM 7-2. NOSE ON THE BALL – TAKE CHARGE AT HALF COURT (CONTINUED)

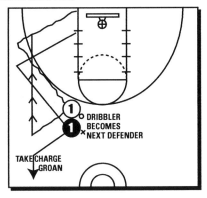

- O1 makes a move, taking three dribbles to his left

- X1 guards O1, staying down in a defensive stance

Diagram 7-2c.

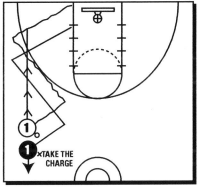

- O1 makes a move and dribbles toward half court

- X1 beats O1 to a spot just before half court

- X1 establishes position

Diagram 7-2d.

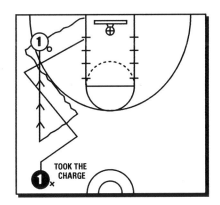

- X1 takes the charge on O1

- O1 turns with the ball and passes it back to the next offensive player who is waiting at the baseline

- O1 sprints to guard the next offensive player

Diagram 7-2e.

DIAGRAM 7-3. HERDING – THREE DRIBBLES AND TRAP

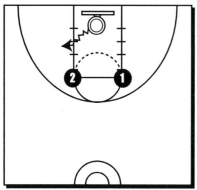

Diagram 7-3a.

- O1 starts with the ball in the middle of the court

- X1 and X2 are at the elbows in a good defensive stance

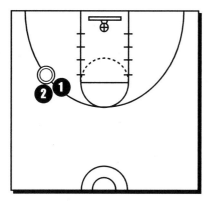

Diagram 7-3b.

- O1 takes three explosive dribbles to his right

- X2 beats O1 to a spot, cutting off the sideline

- X1 herds O1 from the back, guarding the middle

- O1 picks up the dribble

- X1 and X2 trap O1 with their hands held high and their legs crossed

DIAGRAM 7-4. HERDING – ZIG-ZAG DRIBBLE AND TRAP

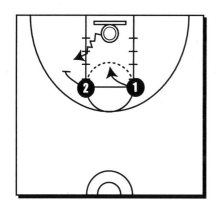

Diagram 7-4a.

- O1 starts with the ball in the middle of the court

- X1 and X2 are at the elbows in a good defensive stance

DIAGRAM 7-4. HERDING – ZIG-ZAG DRIBBLE AND TRAP(CONTINUED)

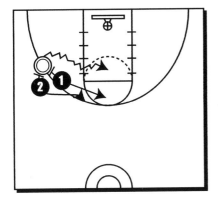

Diagram 7-4b.

- O1 takes three explosive dribbles to his right

- X2 beats O1 to a spot, cutting off the sideline

- X1 herds O1 from the back, guarding the middle

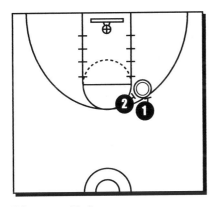

Diagram 7-4c.

- O1 makes a move, takes three explosive dribbles to his left

- X1 beats O1 to a spot, cutting off the sideline

- X2 herds O1 from the back, guarding the middle

- O1 picks up the dribble

- X1 and X2 trap O1 with their hands held high and their legs crossed

DIAGRAM 7-5. HERDING – ZIG-ZAG DRIBBLE, TRAP AND CHASE

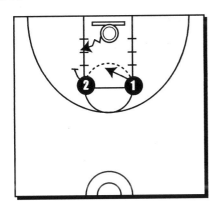

Diagram 7-5a.

- O1 starts with the ball in the middle of the court

- X1 and X2 are at the elbows in a good defensive stance

DIAGRAM 7-5. HERDING – ZIG-ZAG DRIBBLE, TRAP AND CHASE (CONTINUED)

Diagram 7-5b.

- O1 takes three explosive dribbles to his right

- X2 beats O1 to a spot, cutting off the sideline

- X1 herds O1 from the back, guarding the middle

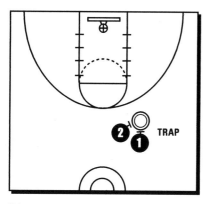

Diagram 7-5c.

- O1 makes a move, takes three explosive dribbles to his left

- X1 beats O1 to a spot, cutting off the sideline

- X2 herds O1 from the back, guarding the middle

- O1 picks up the dribble

- X1 and X2 trap O1 with their hands held high and their legs crossed

Diagram 7-5d.

- O1 passes out of the trap to the coach

- X1 and X2 sprint out of the trap and chase the coach from behind, tying to prevent him from shooting a lay-up

DIAGRAM 7-6. HERDING – 3-ON-3

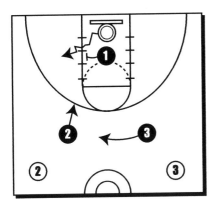

Diagram 7-6a.

- O1 starts with the ball in the middle of the court
- X1 guards O1 in a good, low defensive stance

- O2 and O3 are positioned near half court

- X2 and X3 are "up the line", anticipating trapping the dribbler

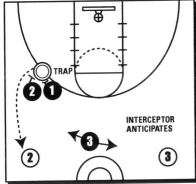

Diagram 7-6b.

- O1 takes three explosive dribbles to the right

- X1 plays "nose-on-the-ball" defense against O1

- X2 moves forward to "slow trap" O1

- O1 picks up the dribble

- X1 and X2 trap O1 with their hands held high and their legs crossed

- X3 rotates to the middle, anticipating the next pass

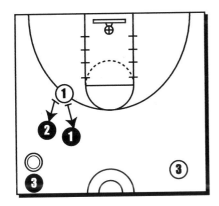

Diagram 7-6c.

- O1 passes the ball to O2 at half court

- X3 then rotates to pick up O2

- X1 and X2 sprint out of the trap, converting quickly to defense

DIAGRAM 7-7. ANTICIPATION DRILL

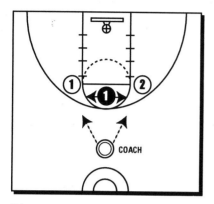

Diagram 7-7a.

- O1 and O2 are positioned at the elbows

- X1 "splits" O1 and O2, in a good, low defensive stance

- X1 anticipates the pass to either O1 or O2

- The coach has the ball 15' away

Diagram 7-7b.

- The coach makes the pass to O2

- X1 attempts to deflect or steal the pass to O2

Diagram 7-7c.

- O2 passes the ball back to the coach

- X1 gets quickly back in position, anticipating the next pass

DIAGRAM 7-8. ANTICIPATION DRILL – "55"

- X1, X2, X3, X4, and X5 are set up in "55", the 1- 2-1-1 full-court zone press

- The coach takes the ball out of bounds

- The coach attempts to inbound to any player – O1, O2, O3, or O4

- X3, X2, X1, and X5 are looking to deflect or steal the inbounds pass

Diagram 7-8a.

- The coach completes the inbounds pass to O1 (or O2)

- One trap occurs and the defense rotates, anticipating the next pass

Diagram 7-8b.

DRILL #4. 2-ON-2 – HELP, DEFLECT, AND RECOVER. (Guard/forward).
(Refer to Diagram 7-9).

- Point guard O1 attempts to make a wing entry to forward O2.
- X1 puts great pressure on O1 and forces him sideline.
- X2 denies O2 the easy entry pass.
- O1 then tries to force help by beating his man off the dribbler.
- X2 helps X1.
- O1 picks up the ball to pass to O2.
- X2 tries to deflect the pass and then recover to his man; we want X2 to recover to O2 and keep him sideline.

* Controlling the drill: limit the number of dribbles to three for the offense; use a "coach" to help defend on a baseline drive.

DIAGRAM 7-9. 2-ON-2 – HELP, DEFLECT, RECOVER

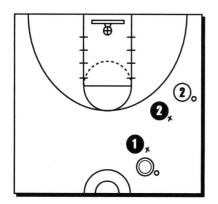

Diagram 7-9a.

- O1 starts with the ball near half court

- X1 pressures O1, forcing him sideline

- O2 is on the wing, looking for the entry pass from O1

- X2 denies the easy entry pass from O1 to O2

Diagram 7-9b.

- O1 beats X1 off the dribble

- X2 opens up to help guard O1 on penetration

- O1 picks up the dribble and makes the pass to O2

- X2 closes quickly and tries to deflect the pass to O2

Diagram 7-9c.

- X2 recovers to O2 and keeps him sideline

- X1 recovers to be in good position to guard O1

DRILL #5. 3-ON-3 – HELP, DEFLECT, AND RECOVER. (A point and two wings).
(Refer to Diagram 7-10).

Same as 2-on-2 but now the offense can initiate on either side of the floor.

Note: Faking on defense is a "must".

DRILL #6. SHELL DRILL. (A point, two wings, one low post set). (Refer to Diagram 7-11).

- We tell each defender, who is guarding a man without the ball, to be "up-the-line and on-the-line." We want our perimeter defense to put great pressure on the ball.

- We want to deny all passes, including any pass to the low post. If a pass is thrown into the low post successfully, we want to attack the low post. We call this "run and stun." We will double or triple team the man in the low post. We will look to deflect any pass out of the post.

- We want our defenders to always see the ball. We want everyone to move in the direction of the ball.

- One key to making the shell drill work properly is the open/close/open/close footwork of the help defense. We want our defenders to constantly work at denying, helping, and denying again, then helping again. To practice these skills, we instruct the offensive players to dribble into the gaps and force a help situation. The defense must then react to the penetration by opening up and helping each other.

- The anticipation of help and recovering is vital. You must develop this as a "habit," not as a reaction. We want to again be the ones "creating the action."

- We want all of our defenders seeing the ball and looking for deflections.

Note: We also use the shell drill with different sets (e.g., two guards and two forwards; ball screen at top of key with two wings).

DRILL #7. WING DENY 2-ON-2. (Refer to Diagram 7-12).

- O1 and O2 start at the blocks.

- X1 and X2 work to deny the wing entry.

- Two coaches are positioned in the guard position passing to each other and attempting to make a wing entry to O1 and O2.

- If O1 or O2 catch the entry, they attempt to score.

- It is important for the defense to stop penetration, force a difficult shot, block out, and rebound.

DIAGRAM 7-10. 3-ON-3 – HELP, DEFLECT, RECOVER

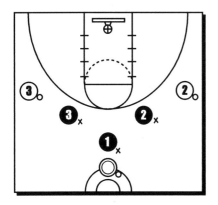

Diagram 7-10a.

- O1 starts with the ball near half court

- X1 pressures O1, forcing him to one sideline

- O2 and O3 are wings, looking for the entry pass from O1

- X2 and X3 deny the easy entry pass from O1

Diagram 7-10b.

- O1 beats X1 off the dribble

- X2 opens up to help guard O1 on penetration

- O1 picks up the dribble and makes the pass to O2

- X2 closes quickly and tries to deflect the pass to O2

- X3 drops into the lane to be in help position

Diagram 7-10c.

- X2 recovers to O2 and keeps him sideline

- X1 recovers to be in good position guarding O1

- X3 is in the lane in help position

DIAGRAM 7-10. 3-ON-3 — HELP, DEFLECT, RECOVER (CONTINUED)

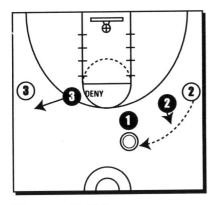

- O2 passes the ball back to O1

- X1 is back pressuring O1

- X2 is back denying the easy pass from O1 to O2

- X3 moves up to deny the easy pass from O1 to O3

Diagram 7-10d.

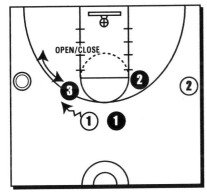

- O1 beats X1 off the dribble

- X3 opens up to help guard O1 on penetration

- O1 picks up the dribble and makes the pass to O3

- X3 closes quickly and tries to deflect the pass to O3

- X2 then drops into the lane to be in help position

Diagram 7-10e.

- X3 recovers to O3 and keeps him sideline

- X1 recovers to be in good position guarding O1

- X2 is in the lane in help position

Diagram 7-10f.

DIAGRAM 7-11. SHELL DRILL – POINT, TWO WINGS, ONE LOW POST

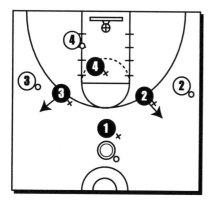

Diagram 7-11a.

- O1 starts with the ball in the middle of the court

- X1 guards O1, pressuring the ball

- O2 and O3 are on the wings

- X2 and X3 are "up-the-line and on-the-line," denying the entry pass

- O4 is set up on the left block

- X4 guards O4

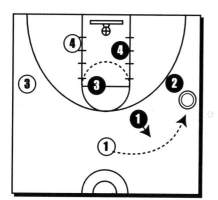

Diagram 7-11b.

- O1 makes the entry pass to O2

- X2 then pressures O2

- X1 denies the return pass to O1

- X3 and X4 move in the direction of the pass into a help position

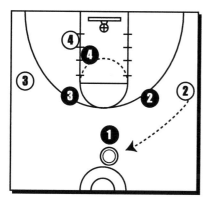

Diagram 7-11c.

- O2 makes the return pass to O1

- X1 is back pressuring the ball

- X2 and X3 are back denying the wings

- X4 guards O4

DIAGRAM 7-11. SHELL DRILL – POINT, TWO WINGS, ONE LOW POST (CONTINUED)

Diagram 7-11d.

- O1 makes the entry pass to O3 on the other wing

- X3 pressures O3

- X1 denies the return pass to O1

- X4 works to deny the post entry pass to O4

- X2 moves into help position

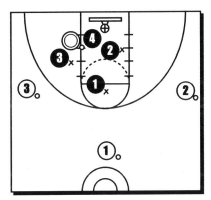

Diagram 7-11e.

- O3 passes the ball to O4 in the post

- X4 works to get himself between O4 and the basket

- X3 and X2 execute the "run and stun" in the low post

- X1 drops into the lane, ready to help on the opposite block

DRILL #8. THE CELTIC DRILL. (Five steps). (Refer to Diagrams 7-13 to 7-17).

Step 1. 4-on-0 – lay-ups only; bank jumpers only; trailer.

Step 2. 4-on-1 – block shot; live.

Step 3. 4-on-2 – live.

Step 4a. 4-on-3 – live.

Step 4b. 4-on-4 – live.

Step 5. 4-on-1 into 4-on-4 press – man; quick trap; slow trap; twist.

Note: In Steps #1, #2, #3, and #4, the ball should not be taken out-of-bounds after a score; in step #5, you take the ball out-of-bounds and play the drill like it's a game.

Step 1. 4-on-0:

A. Players #1, #2, #3, #4 begin the drill. 4 initiates the drill by rebounding a ball tossed off the backboard to himself. 4 then makes an outlet pass to 1. 2 and 3 begin in the corners and fill the lanes on the outlet pass. 1 attacks in transition on the dribble. The first phase is complete when 1 stops his dribble at the top of the key, makes a bounce pass to either 2 or 3, and then shoots a high-speed lay-up off the backboard.

Players A, B, C, D are positioned and ready to take the ball out of the net and continue the drill by having D outlet pass to A, while B and C fill the lanes.

Players W, X, Y, Z are positioned at the other end ready to take the ball out of the net and continue the drill. 4-on-0 continues with high speed lay-ups for two minutes.

B. Same as A, but the players filling the wings do not shoot a high speed lay-up. Instead, the wings shoot a short bank jump shot. Go for one minute.

C. Same as A and B, but instead of the wings shooting, they hold the ball and look for the trailer who runs the middle lane and posts low on the ballside. Go for one minute.

Step 2. 4-on-1:

A. We now add one defensive player from each team who is instructed to stop the dribbler and then try to block the shot when the wings shoot a high-speed lay-up. Do not foul on the shot block attempt.

B. At this point, play live in a 4-on-1 situation. The defense attempts to stop the offense any way it can. We want our defenders to fake at the ball, but guard the basket. The defenders anticipate passes and look to take the charge. Score is kept. The first team to five baskets wins. An alternative is to play for two minutes, and the team ahead at the end of two minutes wins. Competition adds an essential, enjoyable element to the drill.

Step 3. 4-on-2:

A. In this step, another defensive player is added to the drill. The defense is back in a tandem, and the offense attacks 4-on-2. We keep score. Three baskets wins or whoever is ahead after a predetermined amount of time (e.g., one or two minutes). We want the defenders to work together and constantly talk about who has the ball and who is guarding the basket.

Step 4. A) 4-on-3; B) 4-on-4 live:

A. At this point, a defender is added to the drill. This offense is encouraged to get the trailer involved and to find the open man. The defense now has three players working together to stop four offensive players. It is very important for them to communicate, help, rebound, and run. Score is kept. The game lasts for two or three minutes.

B. Another defender is incorporated into the drill, and we play 4-on-4 live. The offense should look to post feed as often as possible and look for dribble penetration.

Step 5. 4-on-1 into 4-on-4 press:

A. Each team has its own coach. (You can designate a player/coach). The three teams now complete the drill by playing full-court pressure defense after all scores. The coach designates what defense they will play: man; quick trap; slow trap; or twist. Each team is instructed to attack in transition 4-on-1, and then convert quickly into their press. Because only one defender is used in the drill at this point, the offense will score almost every time. The one defender then must take it out of bounds while his teammates set up in their press attack. The offensive team immediately converts to the full press and defends for two passes. The defense always stops at mid-court. The offensive team now attacks the press and attempts to score 4-on-1 at the other end. Again, we keep score for two minutes, and the team that is ahead at the end of that time wins.

Step 5 is designed to help develop the habit of pressing after scores. It also forces the team to work on its offensive press attack. The defense works very hard to deny the inbounds pass. The defense looks for one trap. The defense stops just short of half-court, so the offensive team can then attack at the other end. If a defensive team steals the ball, it immediately attacks to score, and the drill continues. If the defense scores, it presses again.

We do not execute all five steps of the Celtic drill in any one practice. We usually do four or five, 2-minute segments each day for a total of 10 minutes. However, you can use all five steps, in which case, the total practice time should be 16 minutes. You can also use the Celtic drill at two different times during practice each day.

Perhaps, the best part of the Celtic drill is that you are working both the offense and defense in a fast-paced drill. As such, a variety of offensive and defensive skills (habits) can be developed by this drill. You can also add certain points of emphasis each day. For example; we generally emphasize: two-hand rebounding; bounce passes; bank shots; little or no dribbling; and quick-ball movement on offense. We also emphasize to the defense to see the ball and defend the basket. The defense must not give up easy baskets. The defense must work together and look to help each other at all times. By the same token, the offensive players must learn to come meet the ball when it is passed.

AREAS OF EMPHASIS

OFFENSE	
• Two-hand rebounding • Outlet passing • Filling the lanes (wide) • Ball handler jump stopping at top of key • Bounce pass • Wing men use 45-degree angle for high speed lay-up • Wing men use 45-degree angle for bank jumper	• Trailer, looking to fill low post • Quick ball movement • Inbounds passing • "V" cut to catch inbounds pass • Come meet the ball – call for the ball • Take your time; stay poised in trap • Be strong in trap • Use escape dribble versus trap • Press attack

AREAS OF EMPHASIS

DEFENSE	
• Guard the basket; do not give up a lay-up	• Convert quickly from offense to defense
• Block shot without fouling	• Deny inbounds
• Look to take the charge	• See the ball
• Fake at the dribbler	• Anticipate the pass
• Call ball and basket on 3-on-2	• Trap—hands high, feet crossed
• Communicate, help, rebound, run	• Pursuit – stop at mid-court

DRILL #9. THE UCLA DRILL. (Refer to Diagram 7-18).

One of the areas we like to work on is the 5-on-4 and 4-on-3 situations we see when a team gets through our press and outnumbers our defenders. We believe we can build confidence by practicing 4-on-3 and 5-on-4 situations in order to give the defense the opportunity to realize that it can still be successful even though it is outnumbered.

The rules of the UCLA drill are relatively simple:

Step 1. 4-on-3:

• Three defensive players line up in the 3-second lane. Four offensive players line up outside the 3-point circle. The coach passes the ball to one of the offensive players. At this point, the three defensive players react. Someone must closeout the man with the ball, while the other two defenders get ready to either rebound or closeout on the next pass. The offense moves the ball until it can shoot a 3-pointer. The offensive players have only three options: shoot the 3; pass to a teammate for a shot; or get an offensive rebound. The only shot option is a 3-pointer. Everyone crashes the boards. If the offense gets the rebound, they pass it out.

Scoring:

• 1 point for a basket

• 2 points for a defensive rebound

If the offense scores or the defense rebounds, the ball goes back to the coach and the drill continues. The game is played to 6-10 points.

Step 2. 5-on-4:

• Same as 4-on-3, but a defender and a shooter are added to the drill.

Note: You can also add shot fakes and lay-ups.

DIAGRAM 7-12. WING DENY — 2-ON-2

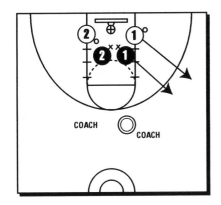

Diagram 7-12a.

- O1 and O2 start on the blocks
- X1 and X2 guard their men in good defensive position
- Two coaches are in guard positions, one with the ball

Diagram 7-12b.

- O1 breaks hard to the 3-point line to catch the ball
- X1 works to deny the pass from the coach to O1
- X2 is in good help position

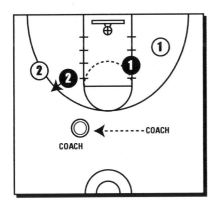

Diagram 7-12c.

- The ball is passed from coach to coach on top
- O2 breaks out, looking to catch the ball
- X2 moves quickly to deny the pass from the coach to O2
- X1 drops off into a help position
- On the coach's pass to O1 or O2, they attempt to score

DIAGRAM 7-13. CELTIC DRILL — 4-ON-0

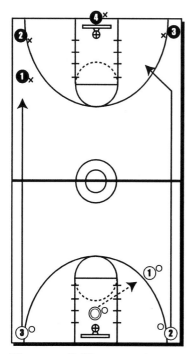

- Team O1-O4 starts at one end of the court

- O4 starts with the ball under the basket

- O2 and O3 start on the baseline

- O1 starts at the foul line extended

- O4 throws the outlet pass to O1

Diagram -7-13a.

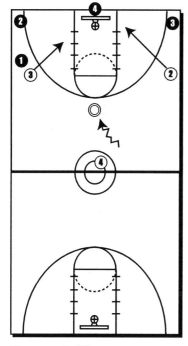

- O1 dribbles the ball quickly up the middle

- O2 and O3 sprint to the foul line extended

- O4 sprints the middle as the trailer

Diagram 7-13b.

DIAGRAM 7-13. CELTIC DRILL – 4-ON-0 (CONTINUED)

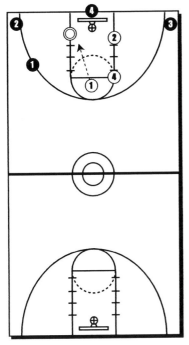

Diagram 7-13c.

- O2 and O3 make sharp cuts to the basket

- O1 passes the ball to O3 for the lay-up

- O4 is in the lane as the trailer

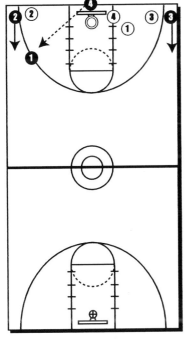

Diagram 7-13d.

- Team X1-X4 is in position at the other end of the court

- O3 makes the lay-up

DIAGRAM 7-13. CELTIC DRILL – 4-ON-0 (CONTINUED)

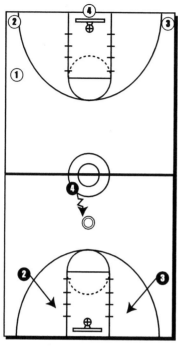

Diagram 7-13e.

- X4 gets the ball out of the net

- X4 then throws an outlet pass to X1

- X1 dribbles the ball quickly up the middle

- X2 and X3 sprint to the foul line extended

- X4 sprints the middle as the trailer

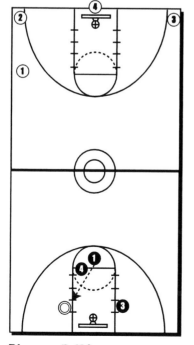

Diagram 7-13f.

- X2 and X3 make sharp cuts to the basket

- X1 then passes to X2 for the lay-up

- X4 is in the lane as the trailer

DIAGRAM 7-14. CELTIC DRILL – 4-ON-1

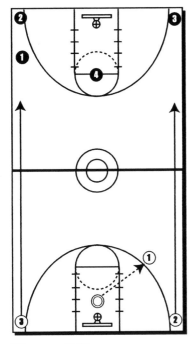

Diagram 7-14a.

- Team O1-O4 starts at one end of the court

- O4 starts with the ball under the basket

- O2 and O3 start on the baseline

- O1 starts at the foul line extended

- O4 throws the outlet pass to O1

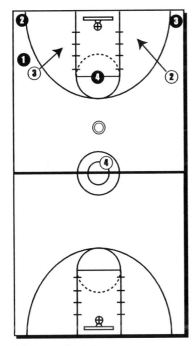

Diagram 7-14b.

- X4 is at the opposite foul line, defending

- O1 dribbles the ball quickly up the middle

- O2 and O3 sprint to the foul line extended

- O4 sprints the middle as the trailer

DIAGRAM 7-14. CELTIC DRILL — 4-ON-1 (CONTINUED)

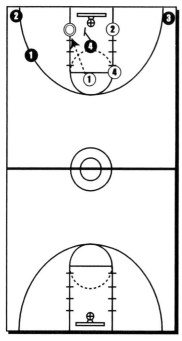

- O2 and O3 make sharp cuts to the basket

- O1 passes the ball to O3 for the lay-up

- X4 drops back to challenge O3's lay-up

- O4 is in the lane as the trailer

Diagram 7-14c.

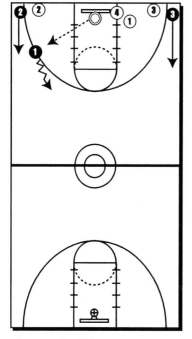

- X1, X2, and X3 are in position at the other end of the court

- O3 makes the lay-up

Diagram 7-14d.

DIAGRAM 7-14. CELTIC DRILL – 4-ON-1 (CONTINUED)

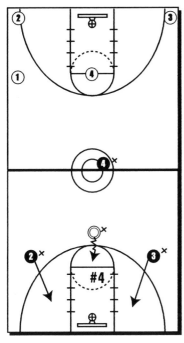

- X4 gets the ball out of the net

- X4 then throws an outlet pass to X1

- X1 dribbles the ball quickly up the middle

- X2 and X3 sprint to the foul line extended

- X4 sprints to the middle as the trailer

Diagram 7-14e.

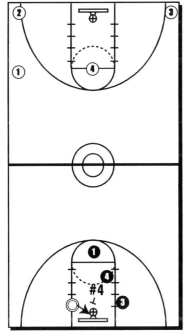

- X2 and X3 make sharp cuts to the basket

- X1 then passes to X2 for the lay-up

- X4 drops back to challenge X3's lay-up

- X4 is in the lane as the trailer

Diagram 7-14f.

DIAGRAM 7-15. CELTIC DRILL – 4-ON-2

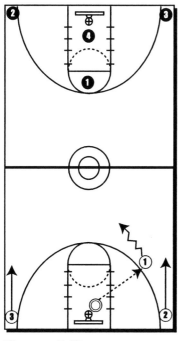

- Team O1-O4 starts at one end of the court

- O4 starts with the ball under the basket

- O2 and O3 start on the baseline

- O1 starts at the foul line extended

- O4 throws the outlet pass to O1

Diagram 7-15a.

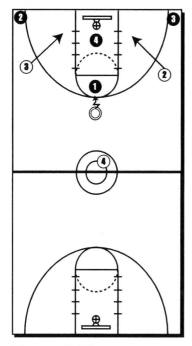

- X1 and X4 are in a tandem, defending

- O1 dribbles the ball quickly up the middle

- O2 and O3 sprint to the foul line extended

- O4 sprints the middle as the trailer

Diagram 7-15b.

DIAGRAM 7-15. CELTIC DRILL – 4-ON-2 (CONTINUED)

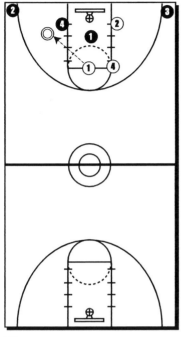

Diagram 7-15c.

- O2 and O3 make sharp cuts to the basket

- O1 passes the ball to O3 on the wing

- X4 takes the first pass and guards O3

- X1 drops into the lane

- O4 is in the lane as the trailer

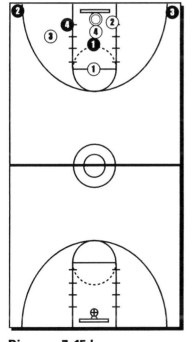

Diagram 7-15d.

- X2 and X3 are in position at the other end of the court

- O3 takes the short jump shot

- X4 and X1 are in position to rebound

- O4 and O2 work for the offensive rebound

DIAGRAM 7-15. CELTIC DRILL – 4-ON-2 (CONTINUED)

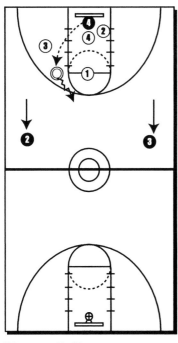

- X4 gets the ball out of the net and then throws an outlet pass to X1

Diagram 7-15e.

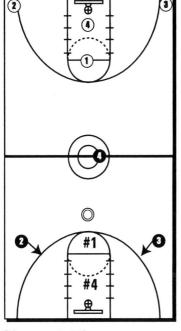

- X1 dribbles the ball quickly up the middle

- X2 and X3 sprint to the foul line extended

- X4 sprints the middle as the trailer

Diagram 7-15f.

DIAGRAM 7-15. CELTIC DRILL – 4-ON-2 (CONTINUED)

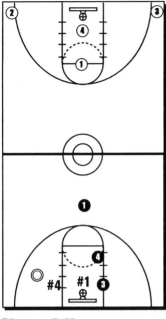

- X2 and X3 make sharp cuts to the basket

- X1 then passes the ball to X2 on the wing

- #4 takes the first pass, guards X2

- #1 drops into the lane

- X4 is in the lane as the trailer

Diagram 7-15g.

DIAGRAM 7-16. CELTIC DRILL – 4-ON-3

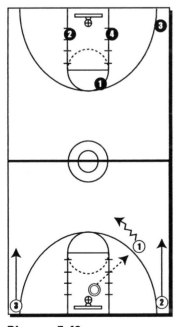

- Team O1-O4 starts at one end of the court

- O4 starts with the ball under the basket

- O2 and O3 start on the baseline

- O1 starts at the foul line extended

- O4 throws the outlet pass to O1

Diagram 7-16a.

DIAGRAM 7-16. CELTIC DRILL – 4-ON-3 (CONTINUED)

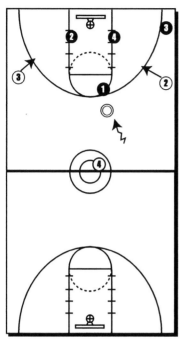

Diagram 7-16b.

- X1, X2, and X4 are defending

- O1 dribbles the ball quickly up the middle

- O2 and O3 sprint to the foul line extended

- O4 sprints the middle as the trailer

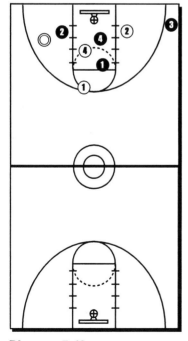

Diagram 7-16c.

- O2 and O3 make sharp cuts to the basket

- O1 then passes the ball to O3 on the wing

- X2 takes the first pass, guards O3

- X4 comes across the lane to help

- O4 is in the lane as the trailer

DIAGRAM 7-16. CELTIC DRILL – 4-ON-3 (CONTINUED)

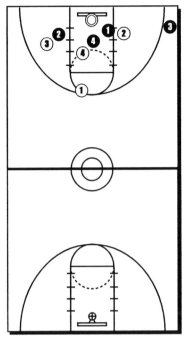

- X3 is in position at the other end of the court

- O3 takes the short jump shot

- X4, X2, and X1 are in position to rebound

- O4 and O2 work for the offensive rebound

Diagram 7-16d.

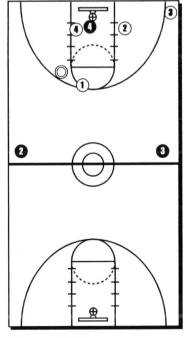

- X4 gets the ball out of the net and throws an outlet pass to X1

Diagram 7-16e.

DIAGRAM 7-16. CELTIC DRILL – 4-ON-3 (CONTINUED)

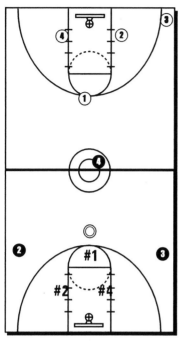

- X1 dribbles the ball quickly up the middle

- X2 and X3 sprint to the foul line extended

- X4 sprints the middle as the trailer

Diagram 7-16f.

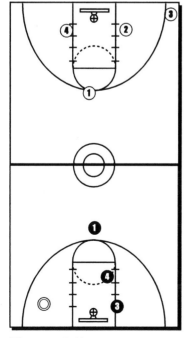

- X2 and X3 make sharp cuts to the basket

- X1 then passes the ball to X2 on the wing

- #2 takes the first pass, guards X2

- #4 comes across the lane to help

- X4 is in the lane as the trailer

Diagram 7-16g.

DIAGRAM 7-17. CELTIC DRILL – 4-ON-4

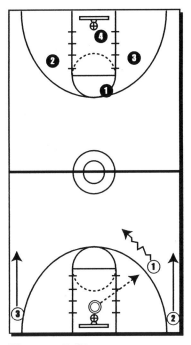

- Team O1-O4 starts at one end of the court

- O4 starts with the ball under the basket

- O2 and O3 start on the baseline

- O1 starts at the foul line extended

- O4 throws the outlet pass to O1

Diagram 7-17a.

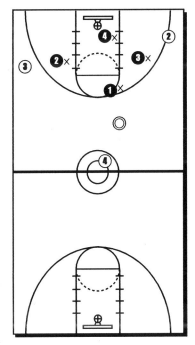

- X1, X2, X3, and X4 are defending

- O1 dribbles the ball quickly up the court

- O2 and O3 sprint their lanes

- O4 sprints the middle as the trailer

Diagram 7-17b.

DIAGRAM 7-17. CELTIC DRILL – 4-ON-4

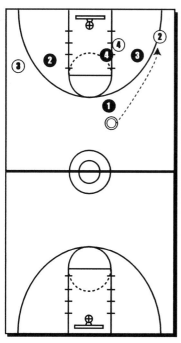

- O2 and O3 get to their transition spots

- O4 runs to the block

- X1 picks up the ball and guards O1

- X4 picks up O4 and guards him in the post

Diagram 7-17c.

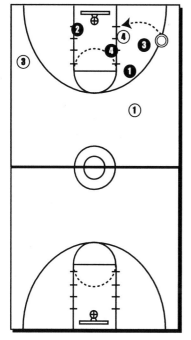

- O1 passes the ball to O2 in the corner

- X3 picks up O2 and guards him in the corner

- X2 drops into the lane to help

Diagram 7-17d.

DIAGRAM 7-17. CELTIC DRILL – 4-ON-4 (CONTINUED)

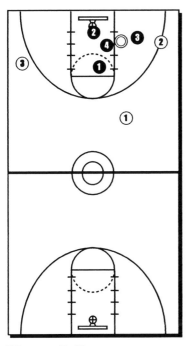

- X4 stays between O4 and the basket

- X2 and X3 "run and stun" on O4, who either takes the shot or passes out

Diagram 7-17e.

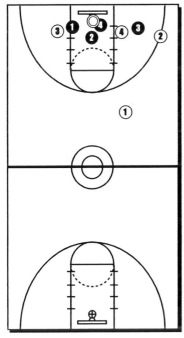

- X1 drops in to box out O3 on the backside

- X1, X2, and X4 are positioned to rebound

- X4 either gets the ball out of the net or rebounds

Diagram 7-17f.

DIAGRAM 7-17. CELTIC DRILL – 4-ON-4 (CONTINUED)

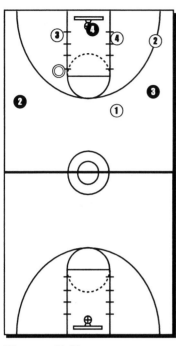

- X4 throws an outlet pass to X1

- X2 and X3 begin to sprint their lanes

Diagram 7-17g.

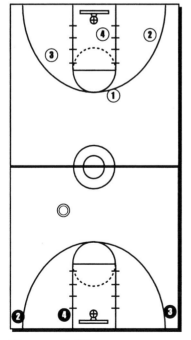

- X1 dribbles the ball quickly up the court

- X2 and X3 get to their transition spots

- X4 sprints to the block

Diagram 7-17h.

DIAGRAM 7-18. UCLA DRILL

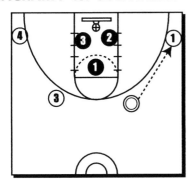

Diagram 7-18a.

- Four offensive players are around the 3-point line

- O2 has the ball

- Three defenders are positioned inside the lane as shown

- The first team to five points wins

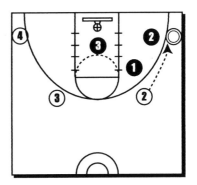

Diagram 7-18b.

- O2 passes to O1 in the corner

- X2 guards the ball

- X1 steps out to anticipate a passback to O2

- X3 prepares to play the skip pass to O3 or O4

Diagram 7-18c.

- O1 throws the skip pass to O3

- X3 guards O3

- X1 sprints to the ball side, anticipating the pass to O4

- X2 then drops into the lane to rebound the shot or play the return pass

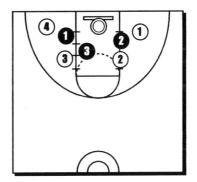

Diagram 7-18d.

- O3 shoots the 3-point shot

- All offensive players go hard after the offensive rebound

- An offensive rebound is kicked out, and the offensive players stay on offense

- A 3-point make is a point for the offense

- A defensive rebound is a point for the defense

8

PREPARATION

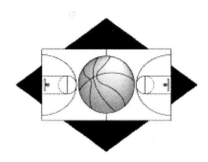

"The best preparation for tomorrow is to do a great job today."

There is nothing more important than good preparation for anything you are about to do. In coaching, this includes preparing for practice each day, for every game and also for all of your travel plans for away games. It is important to look at each area and plan for the entire season. We want to establish as many routines as possible. The preparation for each practice, home game, and away game is as similar as we can possibly make it.

Practice preparation begins long before the season ever starts. Practice planning begins with your philosophy and style of play. It is important for you and your staff to get together before the season and create the vision that you are looking for your players to implement during the year. It is important to make a list of priorities, plus a schedule for introducing them in practice and organizing your time effectively to get the results you want.

Once you have established your philosophy and style, you can determine the things that are most important and need to be introduced immediately. You must develop a "consistent practice plan" from which you can systematically teach the habits you are looking for in your players. During the season my staff and I meet each morning to go over the day's practice plan. This is very important. We want to be sure that each and every member of our coaching staff is on the same page. In this way, we all will be using the same vocabulary, the same terminology, and emphasizing the same teaching points. There is nothing more difficult for a player to adjust to than hearing the same thing said two different ways from the coaches. For example, if one of your coaches instructs a player to get "in the lane", does he mean the passing lane or the three-second lane? We want to use words that paint a picture. If the coach wants a player in the passing lane, we expect him to use the word "deny." This one word describes what we want to accomplish without any confusion.

Practice preparation also includes how you want to utilize your staff. For us, three assistant coaches are assigned specific areas of concentration much like a football staff. Mike Gillian is our offensive coordinator. Bill Courtney is our defensive coordinator. Scott Cherry is in charge of our scout team. During practice drills these coaches watch for their areas of emphasis. We want all of our coaches to coach both offense and defense, but when we are into a drill, Coach Gillian keeps a close eye on the offense and Coach Courtney watches the defense. Coach Cherry works very closely with our second unit to be sure that they are executing the opposing team's offense and defense correctly.

As the head coach, I oversee all of the drills. Once we get into five-on-five team play, I coach the first unit along with Mike and Bill. Scott then takes over the scout team and they execute the opponent's game plan.

GAME DAY

It is very important to establish certain pre-game rituals. We want our players to get themselves in the proper mental frame of mind to play. For home games, we always have a shoot-around five hours before game time. We stretch, warm up, shoot, and go over any last-minute instructions. However, at this point, we do not want to burden our players with a lot of additional information that might prove to be confusing. If we haven't covered a particular topic by this point, we feel we are better off leaving it out. Too much information can create hesitation on the court. During the shoot-around, we want our players to feel good. As such, we try to create an upbeat atmosphere that will help them play their best. The shoot-around lasts approximately 45 minutes. Afterwards, we shower, change, and dress as a team in our George Mason travel warm ups. We want our team looking as one, thinking as one, and acting as one. We then eat our pre-game meal as a team.

Each player is required to arrive at our home arena, the Patriot Center, an hour and 15 minutes before games. If a player needs attention from our trainer, his schedule will include a stop at the training room. The players are dressed and ready to play one hour before tip off. They each shoot on their own, stretch on their own, and put themselves in the proper mental frame of mind to play the game. Forty-five minutes before the game, we meet as a team. Everyone gathers around the grease board to read the scouting report and listen to an upbeat song, which helps create a positive atmosphere in the locker room.

Forty minutes before game time, we begin our pre-game talk. First, our scout team coordinator goes over the opponent's personnel and their offensive and their defensive game plan. Next, our defensive coordinator goes over our defensive assignments, including any specific areas of emphasis. Then, our offensive coordinator gives the players our game plan with a strong emphasis on attacking the basket and getting to the foul line.

Last, I address the team and make one or two points that I feel are the most important to win this game. Our entire pre-game routine takes 15 minutes.

Thirty minutes before tip off, our team takes the floor for our warm-ups. We have a set routine of two line lay-ups, three line lay-ups, passing, dribbling, shooting, and individual defense incorporated into our pre-game warm up. With 12 minutes remaining on the game clock, we return to the locker room for last-minute instructions. At this time, we confirm the starting line up and match-ups and go over our defensive alignments against the opponent's out-of-bounds plays. Then we have a moment of silence before we bring our hands together for one last huddle.

At half-time, we also have a set routine. The players sit in the locker room getting something to drink and discussing the first half amongst themselves. The coaches have a staff meeting and go over the various first-half statistics that are important to us in this particular game. We want to know how many turnovers we've forced. How many rebounds do we have? How many free throws have we attempted? What is the foul situation?

It is very important after our coaches meet at half-time that we go into the players with a clear picture of what we want to accomplish in the second half. We discuss the first half, and make some key points. The most important thing, however, is to really establish the plan for the second half. We want our players leaving the locker room upbeat and excited about playing the second half.

There are occasions when a good tongue-lashing may be required. If you are disappointed in your team's first-half performance and feel you must chastise them to get their attention, this is certainly an appropriate instance. Keep in mind, however, that your ultimate objective is to do whatever you have to do to pull your team together at half-time to get them focused and energized for a great second half.

After the game, a few short comments are appropriate. If you won, it's especially important to celebrate so that the team can feel good about what it accomplished. If you won, but didn't play particularly well, there will be plenty of time to make adjustments before the next game. If you lost, and your team is clearly down, it is important for you to read their body language and act appropriately. Kicking them while they are down may not produce the results for which you are looking. In fact, taking your frustration out on your team may actually create more of a problem.

The skilled coach knows how to motivate and can usually find the right words to focus everybody's attention on one single key point. It may be effort. It may be execution. It may simply be attitude. Whatever it is, the coach should point it out and look toward correcting it immediately, before leaving the locker room. Often, the best time to address a disappointing loss is at practice the next day. Everyone has had time to regroup and get focused again. Making positive steps in practice is often the best preparation for your next game.

AWAY GAMES

Determining how a team plays on the road involves so many factors that you need to take each of them into consideration. For example, it is very important for your travel plans to be made well ahead of time. At George Mason, our travel arrangements are made months ahead, including all our meals, our transportation (bus or plane or both), and hotel accommodations. We want to travel in a first-class manner and as comfortably as we can. The players should be relaxed enough to really enjoy the trip and be looking forward to the game.

On bus trips we often bring movie videos for the players to watch. They either watch the movie or sleep during a two-or three-hour bus trip. We normally bring sandwiches and drinks along so that we do not have stop along the way.

Our managers have a very important responsibility when we travel. They bring all of our equipment – camera, tripod, VCRs, basketballs, etc. so that we have everything we need on the road. We always bring our own basketballs in case the other team does not provide them. Too many times, we have arrived at an arena to find out that the balls are locked up and that their manager does not have the key.

We like to practice at home, if possible, the day before an away game. Because we have control of our own arena and practice times, we don't have to concern ourselves about a possible miscommunication between our staff and our opponents. However, we always schedule a shoot-around the day of the game so that it is consistent with our preparation for games whether it be at home or away.

The night before an away game, we have a team meeting at 10:00 p.m. We go over our game plan, watch an edited tape of our opponent and ourselves, and make sure that everyone knows the schedule for the next day. At this point, being relaxed and confident is our primary goal.

Controlling things you can control and not worrying about the things you can't control is the key to being in the right mental state once you take the floor to play the game that night. Something is bound to go wrong on the road. Maybe the hotel is not ready for you to check in when you arrive. Maybe the showers have no hot water. Maybe there are no basketballs when you arrive at the shoot-around. Whatever the distraction may be, however, it is important for your team to realize that that will only impact the game if you allow it to. Keeping a cool, calm and collected attitude is a much more positive approach to a game, regardless of circumstances beyond your control.

One night, my Bowling Green team played at Western Michigan. Western Michigan's arena was under construction. Our game was moved to their ice arena. When we showed up for our shoot-around, we had a brief team meeting before we took the floor. It was freezing in arena. I said that very few teams would play well under these circumstances and that this was a perfect opportunity for us to beat a team on the road that was not likely to lose many home games because of these adverse conditions. I said "most teams will come in here and use the cold as an excuse to lose. We're going to use it as motivation to win." That night our team played perhaps one of its best games of the season. It was freezing. But we did not let it bother us. We executed our game plan to perfection and came away with a big win.

PREPARATION FOR THE SCRAMBLE VERSUS DIFFERENT SETS

One of the most important aspects of teaching The Scramble is to teach your players how to anticipate their moves based on the various sets they will see from game to game and even from one stage of a game to another. It is vitally important for players to recognize when they are a trapper, an interceptor, or the goaltender. If they are not schooled properly, you may end up with three trappers or three interceptors and no goaltender because all of your players want to steal the ball.

You should remember that The Scramble's primary function is to take an opponent out of its normal rhythm. We want the opponent to react to us. Therefore, we practice our Scramble defense against various sets each week during the pre-season, and against the specific sets we will see in our next game. Proper preparation develops confidence. We do not want any player to have doubt or be hesitant.

The first set in which we teach the half-court Scramble is the 1-2-2. We want a point, two wings, and two low posts. This way, the defense is symmetrical, and everyone can learn the ballside and helpside at the same time by just alternating where the point guard enters the ball.

Once we have taught the basic principles of Thumbs Down and Thumbs Up and are confident of our players, we move directly to the most popular sets we see in our league:

- 3 out, 2 in (1-2-2 set with a point guard, two wings, and two low posts)
- 1-3-1 set with a high-ball screen
- Box set with a dribble entry
- 4 out, 1 in (two-guard set, with two forwards and one low post)
- 2-1-2 set (two guard set, with two forwards and one high post)
- 1-4 high
- 1-4 low into flex
- Double stack low

We practice The Scramble versus each set each week. Since we normally practice five or six days a week, we usually cover two sets each practice session. We want to develop good defensive habits.

In order to develop good defensive habits, we adhere to the following rules:

- Switch all perimeter-on-perimeter screens; switch all post-on-post screens.
- Trap all ball screens.
- Sprint out of all traps; be prepared to rebound.
- Trap all baseline drives.
- Front all low-post players.
- Trap any pass into the post.
- If we steal and score, we stay with the same defense.

FULL-COURT SCRAMBLE VERSUS PRESS ATTACK

In the full-court Scramble, there are three basic offensive sets that we must be prepared to defend:

- 1-2-2: One man out-of-bounds; two men, normally guards, at the elbows; and two men at mid-court, one near each sideline.

- 1-1-2-1: One man out-of-bounds. One man to receive the entry pass at the foul line; two men are at mid-court, one near each sideline; and one man down the court near his basket.

- Four men across the foul line, with all four players being options for the inbounds pass.

In a full-court situation, we want to be certain that we match up quickly no matter what offensive set is being used. As such, it is vitally important for the defensive players to begin communicating as to the role that they're going to assume (i.e., who is going to be the trapper, the interceptor, and the goaltender). Only constant practice enables your players to develop the ability to make this conversion quickly and confidently.

Be certain that when you practice against each press attack, you emphasize denying the inbounds pass, whenever possible, and contesting every pass if you can't deny. Putting immediate and constant pressure on the ball and its first likely receiver helps make the full-court Scramble very effective. You should not play conservatively at this point. Your players can learn the other team's press attack in one day. Most teams have only one press attack. Once you know it, anticipating passes and making good defensive plays become a habit.

GAME SITUATIONS

One of the questions I often get asked by high school coaches is "When should I use The Scramble?" The answer is not so simple. There are many factors that determine when and how much to use The Scramble. The most important question is "How committed are you to pressure defense?" If you are 100 percent committed, you need to begin with your man-to-man defense and be sure your players are working hard to put constant, relentless pressure on the ball. Since we are totally committed to The Scramble, we use it in conjunction with our man-to-man and Scramble full-court or half-court every time we score. The quicker we are, the more we extend the defense and play full-court. The bigger or slower we are, the more we reduce the length of our rotations and Scramble only at the half-court level. If you want to use The Scramble as a change up or only on special situations, you should Thumbs Down after the following instances: time outs, so you can be organized; after made free throws, so you can huddle and communicate better with your team; or when your team needs a quick spurt to get things going in your favor.

If you want to Scramble more, you can develop a system that has additional automatics. For example, you can Scramble on all situations involving the following: ball screens; baseline drives; side out-of-bounds; free throws; time outs; at the end of the half or the quarter when the other team is holding for one shot; and at the end of the game when you're trailing by three or more.

If a team is playing very well against your man or zone, and you want to change the tempo, The Scramble is a perfect defensive alternative. You can choose either Thumbs Down, the most conservative element or Thumbs Up, if you want to get more pressure on the ball handler. You may even want to go to any of the full-court Scramble defenses to put immediate pressure on the ball.

One of the factors involving the Scramble that we have learned over the years is how to effectively use our bench. Two key ways to utilize your bench with The Scramble are:

1.   Your bench can "coach" your defense. By applying half-court pressure in the first half when your defense is in front of your bench, the players on the sideline can communicate with their teammates on the floor. They can remind their teammates to rotate or trap because the action is right in front of them. In the second half, when your half-court defense is away from your bench, you can go to the full-court Scramble. Again, your bench can help get your defense set quickly. It amazes me how much our tenth, eleventh, and twelfth man stay focused and ready to play because they feel they are contributing even when they're on the sideline. This step also helps prepare them mentally when they are called upon to go into the game. Everyone contributes. It is a Total Team Effort. We often see coaches up on the sideline directing traffic, but with your bench players doing the reminding, you (as a coach) can actually relax more and focus more on results.

2.   Our substitution pattern can be very important when we employ The Scramble. As such, it is desirable, although not imperative, to have depth. We want our starters to create the intensity that we look for to start the game. Then, after applying relentless pressure on the ball for four or five minutes, we substitute. We normally like to sub three players at a time. Our point guard, one wing, and one post player come out, replaced by a new group to provide energy in order to keep the defensive intensity high. Utilizing eight, nine or 10 guys also keeps your bench into the game. Having depth can help you overcome foul trouble or injuries during a game or season.

Most high school coaches, especially those coaching at the freshman and junior varsity level, need to utilize their bench. At that stage of competition, the top two or three players are often better than the other players on the team. From player 4 to 10, however, there is probably very little difference. Giving young players *some* playing time will help sustain their interest, help keep them motivated, and eventually may help them develop into productive players. Every good high school program makes a concerted effort to develop its young talent. Sitting on the bench, game after game, with no playing time in sight can discourage even the most enthusiastic young player.

Games are basically a test. They test how well a coach has prepared his team in practice to execute under game conditions. They also test how well a player has learned his lessons and whether he is capable of performing against others – including very tough competition.

We believe that our drills teach the necessary skills to our players. The constant repetition develops the habits and instincts to perform under all conditions. Our competition in practice, scrimmages and mini-games provides the necessary dress rehearsal for what our players can anticipate under game conditions. We even bring in referees to work our practices during the preseason. This step makes the practices and the scrimmage games as close to realistic as possible.

Under game conditions, we utilize The Scramble after all made field goals and all made free throws. We have created this habit through constant repetition. Our players are mentally focused on being able to pressure the opponent relentlessly for the full 40 minutes.

We also practice converting from offense to defense after a missed field goal or a missed free throw. In both of these cases, we convert to our man-to-man defense. Because we feel that our defensive conversion to man-to-man is vitally important, this aspect is always an area of emphasis. We do not want to give up easy baskets in transition to our opponent as we convert from offense to defense. Constant drilling and frequent reminders help our players focus on and successfully execute this very important aspect of the game.

DON'T SCRAMBLE

Is there ever a time when your team shouldn't Scramble? In fact, there may be very specific situations that you do not want to Scramble. For us, these are few and far between. When an opponent is attacking our full-court Scramble well, then we know we need to make an adjustment. However, this adjustment never involves taking The Scramble off completely. In these circumstances, we switch from the full-court Scramble to the half-court Scramble. In that situation, we trap either at half-court or at the wing. Our emphasis is still on pressure and trapping.

There are times, however, when we choose not to Scramble. For example, if the score is tied with less than 30 seconds in a game and we are on defense, we may elect to play straight up man-to-man. Man-to-man is still our bread and butter defense. We believe that we can get one stop and rebound the ball. After we've stopped them, we then call an immediate timeout to set up a last second shot for ourselves. One reason that we may decide not to Scramble with the score tied at the end of a game is because we want to avoid the possibility of a foul. Officials tend to call fouls in traps – especially when you are on the road.

Another reason we may elect not to Scramble involves the fact that if there is a timeout, we often change our defense on the last possession. This step frequently causes the opposing coach to call an additional timeout. Keep in mind that how much and when to utilize The Scramble is something that each coach has to decide for himself. As such, you have to be comfortable with your decisions. You have to have confidence that your players can execute The Scramble. No matter what defense you choose to play, the most important thing is to play it well. Furthermore, your players must believe in their defense.

9

PRACTICE

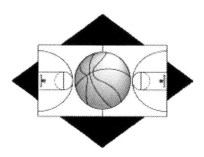

We have developed a practice plan over the years that works well for us. It is important for a coaching staff to establish a practice style and practice routines with which your players feel comfortable. Table 9-1 illustrates the daily practice plan that we employ at George Mason.

We begin by posting our practice plan each day on the locker room bulletin board. Each player is required to read the plan, so he knows what to expect. At the top of the practice plan, we post the four names of the group leaders for the day. The group leaders are responsible for serving as demonstrators for any drill that we run that practice. We expect them to hustle to the starting point and get the team going quickly. We believe that you develop and train leadership just like any other skill. If you want an individual to be a leader, then you must put him in a leadership role on a regular basis for him to develop confidence. By assigning different players each day to be group leaders, we identify the best leaders on the team.

We also have a "Thought of the Day" at the top of our daily practice plan. Each player is required to memorize the "Thought" and be prepared to recite it at practice, if asked. The "Thought" is either motivational, inspirational, or fundamental. We want our players thinking as "one" and we believe that you can get your team on the same page to start each practice with a "Thought of the Day" that gets them focused.

Once we take the practice floor, the players know the whistle will blow at the precise time we intend to start practice. When the whistle sounds, each player should immediately take his ball and put it in the ball rack and then meet the others at the mid-court circle. We gather around the mid-court circle, players and coaches standing shoulder to shoulder, forming a united circle. The significance of this circle is for everyone to realize that we are all in this together, working together. While each person has his own responsibilities, we all impact each other. We are interdependent. We must work in unison to be successful.

The group then begins clapping in unison. The clapping ends when I count back... "3,2,1." At the precise moment that I have counted "1", the clapping stops. We then ask one player to recite the "Thought of the Day." At this point, we emphasize how important it is to practice well. Next, we huddle, putting all of our hands in and chanting "together!" We also end the practice session with a huddle at mid-court and the chant "together." We believe that the players form a bond throughout the season by ritualizing the start and end of practice.

RITUALS

As you can tell, we believe in rituals. We are not the only ones. For example, John Wooden spent one afternoon before the start of each season showing his players how he wanted them to put on their socks and shoes to avoid getting blisters. Each UCLA player was required to put his socks and shoes on the same way everyday. This step had a physical benefit, but more importantly a mental benefit, too. The UCLA players knew that after putting their shoes on they were "ready to play."

Michael Jordan played every game of his career with the Chicago Bulls wearing his North Carolina practice shorts under his uniform. Did Jordan need those shorts on to play well physically? Absolutely not! He wore them for good luck. He wore them as part of his ritual for preparing to play. Jordan also ate the same pre-game meal before every game. He wanted his body and mind to be in sync.

Jerry Rice, the All-NFL wide receiver for the San Francisco 49ers, dresses exactly the same way for practice as he does for games. He always has his ankles taped exactly the same way, first the right ankle then the left. He always puts on his gear in exactly the same order, neatly and precisely.

Putting yourself in the proper mental frame of mind to play requires preparation. Rituals help to systematically put you "in the zone." We believe that by developing these routines, they become a part of who you are. As such, routines and rituals can be a big part of developing a winning tradition. Tables 9-5, 9-6, and 9-7 present an overview of our pre-game player routine, pre-game warm-up routine, and post-game thoughts, respectively.

As part of our rituals, we begin every practice with a segment of fundamental drills. This step helps our players to warm-up properly and focus on executing the fundamental skills of basketball. The first part of practice also includes our defensive drills because the players tend to have more energy at the beginning of practice. Table 9-3 presents a menu of the defensive drills that we utilize. This segment of practice is highly intense and competitive. We want the players to concentrate on improving their defensive skills and learning how to play hard everyday. Constant repetition and competition enables each player to improve his defensive ability. If each player improves, then the whole team improves. To build team pride in our team defense, we emphasize it early and often each and every day. A defensive mind-set permeates throughout our practices and our games.

We also believe that it is better to work on our offense toward the end of practice. Because we want to be able to execute at the end of close games, we practice our offense when we are a little tired. By emphasizing our offense toward the end of practice, our players are also forced to concentrate on making their shots when their legs have been put through a two-hour workout. This step helps to simulate game conditions.

During practice sessions, we also include several segments of competitive free-throw shooting. Free throws are probably the single most important aspect of offense at the end of close games. We want our players to be mentally tough and have tremendous confidence when they go to the foul line. They can gain that confidence by making game-winning free throws in practice on a regular basis. Accordingly, they come to believe in themselves in these situations.

We always end practice with stretching, just before we come together one last time around the mid-court circle. Not only does stretching at the end of practice help reduce soreness the next day, it can also improve flexibility. Furthermore, because we always want to leave the floor united, it can have a physical benefit as well as mental.

FREQUENCY/DURATION/INTENSITY

Practice planning also includes understanding the three key categories for determining how to get ready for game days. These categories are:

- Frequency

- Duration

- Intensity

Frequency is the number of times per week you either practice or play. A typical week for us is four practices on Monday, Tuesday, Thursday, Friday, and two games on Wednesday and Saturday with a day off on Sunday.

Duration is the number of hours per practice/game session. Our practices are between one and a half hours to three hours in length. Our practices are longer in November and December, and shorter in January and February. Table 9-4 lists the typical length of a daily practice session over the course of one week.

Intensity is how demanding each practice session is. We expect our practices to be highly intense and competitive. But, we understand that not every drill or segment of practice can or should be at the highest level of intensity. Segments that include elements, such as instruction, a walk through, executing offense without defense, some shooting drills and passing drills, are very light in intensity. In these instances, relatively little physical effort is required. This part of practice is designed to teach skills and concepts. There are also some drills that are fast paced, like fast-break drills, that are conducted at a moderate-level. The players are running hard but only three, four, or five players are involved, while the other players are waiting to rotate in. Drills like 3-on-2 and the 2-on-1 would be considered medium intensity. Half your team is resting while waiting for their turn.

The high-intensity drills are normally either 5-on-5 or 4-on-4 or those when every player is involved, like "nose on the ball." The players are working extremely hard, similar to game conditions. The offensive and defensive players are intensely focused and compete with a "winning attitude."

Practice is designed to have a rhythm. We begin with light/medium warm-up drills. They are followed by highly intense defensive drills. Each defensive segment (normally four minutes in length) is followed by two minutes of shooting. The "rhythmic" practice sequence adheres to the following order of elements: light, medium, high, light, medium, high, etc. (refer to Figure 9-1). A segment can be lengthened or shortened, but the idea is to keep the rhythm. For example, a stand-around "instructional segment" is never followed by a high-intensity segment. After a "walk through", we always warm up again with either a light or medium intensity drill before going full throttle again.

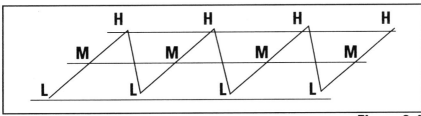

Figure 9-1

WEEKLY PLAN

The most important days of the week are game days. Let's face it, the goal is to play your best in every game. Your practices should be designed to help you do that. Your practice schedule should be planned accordingly so that you are peaking each week on game days. We want to be at our best every Wednesday and Saturday, since those days are when we play most of our conference games. In order to play well, you need to practice well. However, if someone asks me, would you rather play well or practice well, I'd have to choose play well. Our real goal is to both practice well and play well. However, I have seen too many occasions where a team practiced well and then left it all on the practice floor and played very poorly in the game. What can be done to prevent this situation from occuring?

By emphasizing a pattern of practice, we prepare better for game day. For example, consider Sunday. Sunday is always our day off. Dr. Steven R. Covey, in his book, *The Seven Habits of Highly Effective People,* states very clearly that one of the most important habits you can develop is the habit of "sharpening your saw." He explains that it is very important to take a day off and let your mind and body be rejuvenated by resting. He uses the example of two men who are trying to cut down trees by working furiously hour after hour. At the end of the day, one of them has clearly cut down more trees than the other. The second tree cutter asks the first how he was able to cut down so many more trees? The first tree cutter replied, "Every hour I took some time to rest and sharpen my saw!"

We also feel that it is very important to allow your body and mind to rest and relax and become rejuvenated. The energy level that you can produce on game day can be greatly effected by the amount of rest you get leading up to the game. Table 9-6 presents a suggested pattern of intensity for a typical week. Figure 9-1 illustrates how that pattern relates to the weekly practice rhythm.

On Monday, since we have taken Sunday off, we plan our duration and intensity so that we are building up toward Wednesday's game. Football coaches have always followed this approach. Most football coaches start slowly and build toward very intense days in the middle of the week and then shorten the length of practice in order to get ready for Saturday's big game. Basketball coaches should take approximately the same approach but with a different frequency. In basketball, coaches have to plan their practices around two games per week. Therefore, Monday is considered a light/medium intensity day and involves a fairly long practice – two to three hours.

Light intensity refers to drills that are designed for techniques like shooting and dummy offense. It also includes time for a coach to explain strategy and teaching points. It does not mean "little effort." On Monday, we want certain drills, especially defensive and competitive drills, to be highly intense. On the other hand, a practice has plenty of shooting and instructional segments.

On Tuesday, we try to create the intensity we are looking for under game conditions. Tuesday is a high-intensity day. We want our players focused. Therefore, Tuesday's practice is highly intense, but short in duration, lasting about one or one and a half hours. While we want our players to work extremely hard, we do not want to sap them of their energy. High-intensity drills are followed by light-intensity drills (e.g., free throw and jump shooting).

Alternating high-intensity activities with light-intensity action involves a training concept referred to as interval training. Basketball is played in intervals. You play very hard for two or three minutes, and then stop for someone to shoot a free throw. Several fast breaks in a row are followed by a scenario where a team slows down and runs half-court offense. The ball is constantly being taken out of bounds, and the game slows down. These intervals are the focus of our practice efforts. We want to be able to go as hard as we possibly can with high intensity, and then slow things down physically and mentally prepare for the next segment.

Wednesday is game day. Our shoot around is designed to warm up our bodies and put ourselves in the proper frame of mind to play the game that night. We do not want to drain anyone of their energy. However, one relatively brief intense segment can be beneficial. It can get your blood flowing and your competitive juices going.

On Thursday, we repeat the cycle over again. Thursday would be a light-to-medium day to allow our players the opportunity to recover a little bit from the demands placed on them the night before. The practice would last approximately two or three hours, with a strong emphasis on light-intensity shooting drills toward the end. Friday's practice would be a high-intensity day but for a shorter period of time. At this point, we are ready to play our second game of the week, on Saturday. On Sunday we get a chance to rest, and "sharpen our saw"!

It is important to note that after each practice segment of defense, offense, and rebounding, we shoot a set of free throws. Again, we are trying to put our players into game-like situations where they go to the foul line after a high-intensity drill. Developing a productive practice system and successful practice routines can help develop consistency in your players' performance. Figure 9-2 and Figure 9-3 illustrate the rhythmic sequencing of our practices. Table 9-1 provides an example of the sheet we use to develop our daily practice plan.

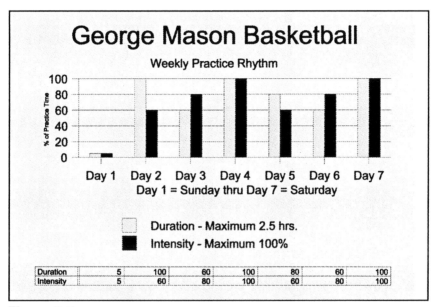

Figure 9-2

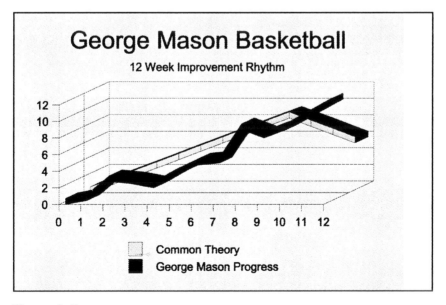

Figure 9-3

MONTHLY PLANNING

In looking at your practice plan for the season, you'll want to be especially focused on peaking at tournament time that typically occurs in late February or early March. Practice planning is then not only week-to-week but also month-to-month. Many coaches subscribe to a common theory that contends that a team can improve steadily throughout the season. Contrary to popular belief, we think there are always peaks and valleys. In this regard, the key is to control those peaks and valleys and to know when they will occur. For example, Figure 9-3 illustrates how we believe teams make the most progress. You'll notice that during the week, you want to be peaking on game day. During the month, you want to set your sights on improving steadily so that you are better at the end of the month than you were at the beginning. Identifying your priorities and constantly working to improve them in each practice can help you accomplish this. The key point to keep in mind is that by the end of the month, your valley should be higher than your peak was weeks earlier. If you then continue that pattern for the next three months, you will be peaking at a much higher level come the end of February. If you don't, you will hit the wall at the beginning of February and start downward as Figure 9-3 clearly illustrates.

PRACTICE PHILOSOPHY

Practice should be fun. In order for practice to be fun, a player must be motivated. He must have a reason to want to practice. Among the positive reasons that can affect why players practice are the following:

- Have fun   - Prepare   - Compete
- Improve   - Win   - Train

When you know why and what your purpose for practicing is, then you have a focus. We want to be known as "The Hardest Working Team in the Country."

Our practice philosophy is to expect 100 percent effort each day. A list of our basic practice session rules is presented in Table 9-2. We want to prepare ourselves physically and mentally for our season and individual games. Practice should be more demanding physically and mentally than an actual game. If this situation occurs, then we know that we have done everything possible to be ready for our opponent. Always keep in mind that if practice is not more demanding than a game, then your opponent may be better prepared, in which case, he will have a clear advantage.

To perform at your highest level you must know what that level is. You must develop the *habit* of playing at that level each day. *Consistency* is the key. Developing the proper habits will enhance your chances of playing consistently.

DAY	SUN	MON	TUES	WED	THUR	FRI	SAT
HOURS	0	2-3	1½	3	2½	1½	3
INTENSITY	0	60	80	100	60	75	100

Table 9-4. Typical daily practice sessions.

These proper habits must be developed to the point where they become instincts. No thought – just action. Confidence at its highest level is reflected by the phrase "Just Do It." The most important ingredient to being successful "under pressure" is confidence.

"Confidence" is the absence of doubt, and the presence of total control. You know you will be successful. You believe in yourself. The best way to develop confidence is to see yourself being successful everyday. Then, when the pressure is on and the time comes to deliver, you fully expect to do well because you do well "all the time, every day, consistently." In other words, "doing well" *is* you.

To do anything well, you must have enthusiasm. You must enjoy doing it. If your goal each day is to improve, then you will concentrate better and stay focused longer. If you just want to get through practice, then you'll not enjoy practicing. As a consequence, you won't improve.

The following five steps should be your prescription on how to approach practice the same way each day:

1. Have fun

2. Be enthusiastic

3. Develop proper habits

4. Focus on improving

5. Give a great effort – mentally and physically

> **"We are what we repeatedly do.**
>
> **Therefore, excellence is not an act but a habit."**
>
> **— Aristotle**

TABLE 9-1. GEORGE MASON BASKETBALL – Daily practice plan.

Date and time:

Group leaders:

Thought of the Day:

I. Stretching (15 minutes)

II. Thought of the Day (3 minutes)

III. Fundamentals (17 minutes)

- •
- •
- •
- •

IV. Defense (50 minutes) – two minutes of shooting after each segment

   A. Conversion

- •
- •
- •
- •

   B. Half-court man-to-man

- •
- •
- •
- •

   C. Scramble

- •
- •
- •
- •

TABLE 9-1. GEORGE MASON BASKETBALL – Daily practice plan. (Continued)

    D.   Full-court defense (man and Scramble)

          •

          •

          •

          •

    E.   Zone defense

          •

  V.   Free throws and water break (3 Minutes)

  VI. Rebounding (12 Minutes)

    A.   Offensive

          •

          •

    B.   Defensive

          •

          •

          • Free-throw rebounding

  VII. Offense (47 Minutes)

    A.   Conversion

          •

          •

          •

    B.   Half-court man

          •

          •

          •

          •

TABLE 9-1. GEORGE MASON BASKETBALL – Daily practice plan. (Continued)

   C. Situations

      •

      •

      •

      •

   D. Zone attack

VIII. Free throws and water break (3 minutes)

IX. Scrimmage/conditioning (15 minutes)

X. Stretching/pull-up trainer (5 minutes)

Total Practice Time (Approximately 3 Hours)

TABLE 9-2. Practice session rules.

- Be on time
- No sitting
- Make eye contact with Coach when he speaks
- Listen to all instructions
- Jerseys must be tucked in at all times
- Players should not offer explanations when given directions from a Coach
- When Coach blows the whistle, everyone stops
- No swearing
- No spitting on the floor
- Be enthusiastic
- Be positive and encouraging
- Have fun
- Keep playing; there is no out of bounds
- If you fall down or get knocked down, get up as quickly as possible
- Group leaders get the team into the next drill before the last drill ends
- If the ball is on the floor, be on the floor

TABLE 9-3. Defensive drill menu.

I.   Pressure ball:

- Nose on the ball – "Pinch"
- Driving line
- Close outs
- Body up/contest (one dribble)

II. Pressure off the ball:

- Wing denial
- Full-court:

        1-on-2

        2-on-2

        2-on-2 Ball screen
- Half-court:

        2-on-2 with down screen

        2-on-2 with ball screen

        2-on-2 with flare screen

III. Help and recover:

- 1-on-2
- 2-on-2
- 2-on-3
- 3-on-3

IV. Rebounding:

- Form
- 1-on-0
- 1-on-1
- 2-on-1
- Superman

TABLE 9-3. Defensive drill menu. (Continued)

- WWII
- WWIII
- 2-on-2 block out/rebound/score

V. Post defense:
- 1-on-1 with ball
- 1-on-1 without ball
- 2-on-2
- 2-on-2 with screens (cross or down):

    post/post

    post/perimeter

VI. Scramble:
- Nose on the ball
- Herding – 2-on-1
- Anticipation drill
- 2-on-2 guard/forward – help and deflect and recover
- 2-on-2 guard/forward:

    Thumbs Down – trap the entry pass

    Thumbs Up – trap the dribbler
- 3-on-3 – point, wing, wing or point, wing, post
- 4-on-4 – point, wing, wing, and post
- 4-on-4-on-4 – transition defense
- 5-on-5 (1-2-2 zone – half-court zone trap)
- Celtic drill
- Conversion drills
- Shell drill
- UCLA drill
- Full-court Scramble drills

TABLE 9-5. Pre-game player routine.

1. We want to dress for practice and games in the same manner:

    - Remove shoes – socks

    - Remove pants

    - Remove shirt

    - Remove and place jewelry away

    - Put on spandex and shorts

    - Put on shirt

    - Sit down – put on socks and shoes

    - Put on warm-up pants, shirt, jacket

2. Music to create the mood: Meditate, prepare – review game plan

3. Pre-game warm-up – repeat simple fundamentals:

    - 2-line lay-ups – one move, finish with a lay-up or floater

    - 3-line weave/lay-up/outlet

    - Two groups:

        guards – shoot

        big men a) one set of nose on the ball

            b) passing – cheat pass, overhead, wrap around

        switch

        everybody shoots with a partner

4. At 12:00, group huddle – captains' comments:

    - Single-tap drill – last player tips it in

    - Quick huddle – then run to locker room

5. Go to the bathroom

    Get a drink

    Grab a seat

TABLE 9-5. Pre-game player routine. (Continued)

6. Five-minute mark – say prayer

    Coach's last instructions

7. Captains' huddle in hallway:

    - Two-line lay-ups

    - :30 huddle

8. Introductions:

    - Form two lines facing each other

    - Huddle

    - Sit in assigned position

10. Game Etiquette:

    - Clap for every basket

    - Stand for every substitution (manager gives towel, jacket, & water)

    - Circle the wagons (subs huddle around coaches during time outs)

    - Players in game surrounded by team

    - Towel – cheerleader – one big man – one guard

11. Free throws – huddle – call play/defense

12 Half-time – run to locker room, drink, sit, talk

13. Time outs – run to bench

14. Address the team

15. End of game:

    - Post-game talk

    - Schedule

16. When leaving the locker room :

    - TAP – play like a champion today!

    - Be sure your shoes are on top of your locker, toes facing back

TABLE 9-6. Pre-game warm-up routine.

I. DRESS   II. TRAINING ROOM – TREATMENT   III. STRETCH

Prior to tip off:

1. 45 Min – everybody seated – start music (rotate who chooses music)
2. 40 Min – Coach Cherry goes over opponent
3. 36 Min – Coach Courtney goes over defensive game plan
4. 34 Min – Coach Gillian goes over offensive game plan
5. 32 Min – Coach L gives last-minute instructions
6. 30 Min – huddle in the hallway; captain speaks (manager – have two balls ready)
7. 28-23 Min – take the floor – two-line lay-ups
8. 23 Min – three lines
9. 21 Min – guards shoot, big men pass (start an area)
10. 18 Min – big men shoot, guards pass (start an area)
11. 15 Min – everybody shoots (walk-ons rebound)
12. 12:30 Min – tip drill – one time through
13. 12 Min – huddle at free-throw line
14. 5 Min – team prayer
15. 4 Min – take the floor
16. 30 Seconds – huddle at the free-throw line
17. Introductions – form two lines
18. Last team huddle

Note: Post this sheet on the bulletin board in the locker room.

TABLE 9-7. Post-game thoughts.

1. Talk about attitude
2. Recognize a sub
3. After a loss:
   - important to find some positive (i.e., we did some good things but we need to execute a little better)
   - no criticism/give credit
   - go over the next day's schedule

WHO AM I?

I am your constant companion,

I am your greatest helper or heaviest burden

I will push you onward or drag you down to failure.

I am completely at your command.

Half the things you do you might just as well turn over to me

and I will do them – quickly and correctly.

I am easily managed – you must be firm with me.

Show me exactly how you want something done

and, after a few lessons, I will do it automatically.

I am the servant of all great people; and, alas, of all failures as well.

Those who are great, I have made great.

Those who are failures, I have made failures.

I am not a machine though I work with all the precision of a machine,

plus the intelligence of a person.

You may run me for profit or run me for ruin –

it makes no difference to me.

Take me, train me, be firm with me and I will

Place the world at your feet.

Be easy with me and I will destroy you.

Who am I?

I am HABIT

– Anonymous

10

COMMUNICATION

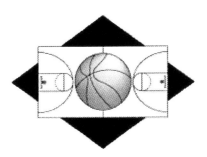

Actions speak louder than words. Did you know that statistically speaking 93 percent of all communication is non-verbal? In other words, body language, facial expressions, eye expression, and other non-verbal communication dominate the way we communicate with each other. This statistic is particularly true in basketball. Have you ever seen a player making a high-speed lay-up and then after scoring, turn and *point* at the man who passed it to him. What does "the point" mean? Everyone knows it means, "thanks, nice pass." Without saying a word, the pass receiver has acknowledged the assist. The passer then lets him know "you're welcome" by nodding his head or pointing back! This form of communication is a must.

On the other hand, have you ever seen a player fumble a nice pass out of bounds, and have the passer look at him in disgust. What is the passer saying without saying a word? "Man, I can't believe you fumbled the ball. What's the matter with you? You blew my assist." Both players drop their heads and pout about it. How much better would it be if they both looked at each other and said, "my fault." The passer would earn a lot of respect by taking some of the blame. Everyone would know whose fault it was, but sharing responsibility for mistakes could contribute to an atmosphere where the importance of teamwork is recognized and accepted.

As coaches, we are responsible for helping players communicate with each other. We have found the best way to do this is to establish certain rituals. For example, after every score, we require the pass receiver to point. It is not optional. At the same time, we require every member of our team to clap for every basket. Cheer for your teammates, on every basket. We also designate at least one guy at the end of the bench to swing a towel. Show your team spirit. Let everyone know you are into the game.

Anytime a player enters the game, the substitute must bring a towel with him. We don't allow long-distance substitutions where the sub just signals who he is going in for. We want contact. When the sub hands the towel to the man he is replacing, they must communicate. The man leaving the game must tell the sub who he is guarding and what defense we are in. Before the sub enters the game, he will have already received instructions from the coaches as to who he should guard. The sub's responsibility is to be sure every teammate on the floor knows who is guarding whom. For example, if a 2 guard subs for a 3 man, the 2 guard must be sure to tell everyone: who he will match up with; and who should cover the 3. Every substitution requires verbal communication among all five players on the floor.

We also require our bench players to stand up and greet every player who leaves the game. Let him know he did a good job. The player must then sit next to one of my assistants and listen for instructions.

TALK

Being a great defensive team demands great communication. Non-verbal communication is not enough. We never want to take anything for granted. Using verbal signals often helps your players execute better. We expect to hear our players "talk" the game throughout the contest. Not trash talk, but teammates talking to each other. When a screen is set, the man guarding the screener must yell "screen right" or "screen left." If someone is helping on a dribbler, the defender must bark out "help left" or "help right." When the other team shoots, we call out, "shot!"

We take this concept one step further in The Scramble. Whenever we trap, we yell "pinch, pinch, pinch." On a dribble pick-up, we call "pinch" or "dead." If a player takes the charge, he must *groan*, and his teammates must run to help him up and pat him on the back or give him a chest bump while the referee is signaling the charge. The body contact again says "good job!" If a perimeter player is screened by another perimeter player, then we call "switch." The point to keep in mind is that communicating well as a team allows you to execute better.

WEEKLY MEETINGS

During the course of the season, we also require each of our players to stop by the office once a week to talk to one of the coaches. We encourage this "off-the-court communication" because we feel it creates the kinds of relationships we need to have with our players to help them be the best that they can be. It also lets us know how they are doing academically, socially, and athletically. As we mentioned, a lot of communication is non-verbal. We can sometimes learn a lot about a player, not by what he says in these meetings, but by what he doesn't say. Is he upbeat? Is he smiling? Often, this information can be very helpful toward "pushing the right buttons" during games.

During the 1998-99 season, we reached a stage in our season where we could easily go one way or the other. We were 9-10, and 6-3 in our league. We had a big home game coming up. We had lost 4 out of 5, including three straight conference games. Our starters were really beginning to feel the pressure. They wanted to win badly. They were giving a good physical effort, but were not being rewarded with a victory. During one of the player/coaches meetings in the office, one of our starters was obviously depressed. "What's wrong?", Coach Gillian asked. "Nothing," the player responded. However, after some prodding, the starter stated that he was not happy about the way he was playing and suggested to Coach Gillian that we take him out of the starting line-up. At the time, it seemed like an innocent comment. The player was frustrated with his own performance. We were searching for answers to help him and his teammates.

Later that day in practice our "Green Team" (the scout team) was just kicking the tar out of the White Team (the starters). The harder the starters tried, the worse they played. The frustration was obvious. The starters were bickering among themselves. The facial expressions and the verbal communication were anything, but positive. Something had to be done. Coach Gillian and Coach Courtney suggested that we change jerseys for the remainder of practice. The Green Team should be the starters, and the White Team should run the opponent's offense. Great suggestion. We did it. But things did not improve.

After practice I called for a team meeting. I felt that something drastic had to be done to snap us out of this funk. I liked my team. They were all good kids. Despite our recent losing ways, I thought we needed just one good win to turn things around.

I began the meeting by telling all of them that they were great kids. That although there was no clear evidence to prove it, I thought we were the best team in our conference. I told them that our Green Team performed magnificently today and throughout the week and season and that I had a lot of confidence in them. I said, "our starters were capable of out-playing anyone on our schedule when they played well together." I told our starters that I had a lot of confidence in them and believed in their abilities. I then said that tomorrow we are going to change roles. The Green Team will start, and the White Team will come in off the bench." With those words every eye in the locker room was glued on me, and the room went deadly silent.

I had learned from my observations that what our team needed more than anything else was to relax and have fun. That's when we played our best. In fact, that's when all teams play their best.

I also told the team that I was not punishing the starters but I was rewarding the Green Team. They were doing a great job. I also said the White Team appeared to be showing some signs of frustration. We should always remember that basketball is supposed to be fun, I reminded them. We should be focused on the process of playing well, not on the prize (winning). We should focus in the present not on the future. Our singular focus should be on playing our best against our next opponent, James Madison. We should not be worried about either the past or the future. Many teams tend to think negatively about the whole year when things are going bad. We just needed to turn this around and begin to think positively again. We wanted our starters to cheer for the Green Team, just as the Green Team had cheered for the starters all season long.

After the meeting ended, I wondered to myself, "What have I done?" The next day, we would have the biggest game of the year. We will have the biggest crowd of the year, 7,000 or more, plus a television audience watching. Our athletic director, the university president, and our most influential supporters would be sitting courtside. What will they think?

I made a call that night to our sports information director, Jim Engelhardt, to let him know our plan. He needed to tell our athletic director, the president, and the television commentators. A surprise like that could be catastrophic. We were going to start our eighth, ninth, tenth, eleventh, and twelfth men in the biggest game of the season. The next day, I arrived at the game smiling. I was happy and confident on the outside. Inside I was nervous, but I knew I couldn't show it.

When the Green Team was introduced, our crowd and our bench went wild. The cheers were deafening. I can't imagine what our opponent was thinking. Not one of our Green Teamers was in their scouting report. They had no clue what was happening. The game began with our Green Team playing defense like a school of hungry piranha. Their intensity was incredible just like we had hoped. After four minutes, the game was tied at 10. The White Team was not sitting still, they were cheering wildly. Their body language was positive. They were ready to play. We substituted as a unit, and as the White team stood, the crowd went wild. The White Team, totally relaxed, entered the game and played like a championship team. The confidence and teamwork were back. Positive energy surrounded us. The Green team was rewarded for their efforts with a short standing ovation from the crowd. We were together again as one.

The game was close and exciting. But a late second-half surge made the difference. By playing 12 players, we had worn down our opponent. The pressure defense paid off by forcing 24 turnovers. We won by just four points. After the victory, the team hustled off the floor and into the locker room. As I entered the room I could hear them chanting "total team effort", "total team effort."

The impact from that victory would effect us the rest of the season. The following game, we faced Old Dominion University. In the pre-season, ODU was picked number one and they were in first place – one game in front of us. It was a "big game," as big as it gets. Taking into consideration that George Mason had never beaten Old Dominion on their home court, we were clearly battling against the odds. The winner would have a big advantage going into the last two weeks of the season and would likely win the regular-season conference championship. The atmosphere in practice was just the opposite of what it had been the week before. Now everyone was smiling, everyone was positive. Everyone's body language spoke volumes of how far we had come in one week. We were ready to play. But Old Dominion was too.

It was a great game. Two teams playing at their best. For 38 minutes Old Dominion was just too good. They led by 4-to-8 points for most of the game. Old Dominion was led by NBA first round draft choice, 6'11" Cal Bowdler, who was basically unstoppable, with 24 points. In fact, with two minutes to play, they led 72-67, and had never trailed. But our pressure defense was still contesting every pass and every shot. We decided to switch from the full-court Scramble to the half-court Scramble. We instructed our players to wait until the ball reached half-court, and then to trap every wing pass and every dribble entry. On the first dribble entry, the dribbler was trapped, and the ball was slapped loose, a quick turnover and a fast break lay-up cut the lead to three points. On the next possession, we trapped again at half court and got another turnover that led to a wide-open three. The stunned crowd was silent. The score was now tied at 72. The intense pressure that they had handled all game long was now forcing turnovers and leading to quick scores. The psychological advantage had turned in our favor. When Old Dominion tried to lob the ball to Bowdler, we fronted and stole the pass. In the last two minutes we out scored Old Dominion 11-2 and won the ball game 78-74.

We went on to win 10 straight games, and the regular-season conference title. The conference tournament was next. We were seeded number one. An NCAA berth would be at stake. A player/coach office meeting between one of our players and assistants had helped immeasurably to set up this improbable finish. Good communication had worked in our favor. Applying this information was about to take us where only one CAA would go – the NCAA Tournament!

11

THE MENTAL GAME

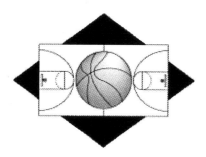

Players need to have a certain amount of physical talent to play the game of basketball suc cessfully. However, physical talent alone is not enough to reach the highest level of competition. We believe the mental and emotional aspects of the game are far more important when you are trying to be the best.

At the highest level of basketball, whether you are coaching high school, college, or professional ball, most teams have a great deal of physical talent. What separates the best from *nearly* the best is, the best teams also show a great aptitude for the mental and emotional side of the game. Most coaches describe players in general terms. They say he's fast, or he's strong, or he's smart. We label players and keep them in that category. We spend a great deal of time trying to enhance each players' physical skills but devote very little time to the improvement of the mental and emotional side of the game. The funny thing is after almost every win, you'll hear coaches say, "We were really well prepared mentally," or "We were really fired up and emotionally energized." It is our belief that we can impact a player's performance more by helping him mentally and emotionally. The best way to help a player is through visualization, and relaxation techniques, both of which help put a player "in the zone."

Accordingly, in our preparation efforts for games, we spend time trying to prepare our players both mentally and emotionally. We talk about how we feel. We talk about feeling confident.

What does it take to feel confident? Having read a lot on this subject, we have shared much of this information with our players. We believe that to be confident you must be in a "good mood." To us, the term "good mood" refers to "feeling positive." We want our players to have lots of energy. We believe that by controlling your thoughts and feelings, you can improve your play mentally and emotionally. In turn, you will enhance your play physically. If you plan on how you will react under the worst circumstances, you can overcome almost any obstacle and be better prepared to win. This concept goes for coaches as well as players. Books like *Peak Performance* by Dr. Charles Garfield and *In the Zone* by Dr. Mitchell Perry deal directly with the overwhelming evidence that great athletes have an edge mentally and emotionally.

How a player handles a mistake or responds to missing a shot can drastically effect his play. As a coach, you can help prepare your players for these inevitable situations. Keep in mind that if a player remains confident, he will likely perform better.

A close friend of mine, Dr. Bob Rotella, taught me the importance of this factor a long time ago. Dr. Rotella is a well-respected sports psychologist, a performance enhancement specialist, and a renowned author of several books on golf. No game is more mental than golf.

Back in 1979, I had the good fortune of getting to know Dr. Rotella and enlisting his help with a problem. We had a player who overreacted every time he missed a shot. So we decided to set up a meeting with Dr. Rotella. In the meeting, Dr. Rotella told him that players with great confidence showed no emotion after missing a shot. Are you a good shooter? Are you confident, asked Dr. Rotella. His answer was, yes. Then the best way to react when you miss a shot is not to react at all. Keep playing. "Try that next game and let me know if it works." The session was over. It was so simple. The player responded very positively. Because he wanted to be perceived as a confident shooter, he was very willing to make the correction.

KNOW YOUR PLAYERS

Many college coaches believe that recruiting is the most important aspect of coaching, and we agree. But the process should not end once a player signs with your school. For us, recruiting and signing a player is just the beginning of the process. We recruit our players every day, over and over again. We don't try to make them feel wanted during the recruiting process and then unappreciated once they arrive at George Mason. Instead, we work at getting to know them. We want to know *what* he thinks and *why* he thinks that way. As previously mentioned, I require each of my players to come by the coaches' office once a week and talk to one of us. We learn a lot about their emotional state during these meetings. Are they feeling good; are they feeling stressed out? If they are feeling stress, what is its source?

On one occasion, one of our players seemed very distracted. He was not shooting well, and he showed very little energy. We found out that he was really struggling with a personal problem. Once we identified the problem, we helped him understand how he could deal with it. Soon after, his shot returned and his performance became more consistent, and soon he was smiling again.

TRUST

We must always remember that basketball is a game and that it should be fun. Players should look forward to practice and games. Helping them prepare emotionally with all the stress they deal with is a key to having a consistent team. The one word that describes this best is "trust." Your players must trust and believe in you, their teammates, and themselves. Such trust is developed over a period of time. You must be able to face some adversity, fail, pick yourself back up, and continue. Don't give up. Keep believing even when everyone else doesn't. Although we would all like to go undefeated, it is not likely to happen.

How *you* handle a loss as a coach is a lot like how a player should handle a missed shot. Don't overreact. Losing is temporary. Get on with what you should do next. Stay mentally tough. Plan your next move. Don't trash your team. A lot of coaches want to place the blame on somebody. Don't fall into that trap. Fix the problem, not the blame. Evaluate, analyze, and communicate. Let your players know what they have to do to play better. Be specific. Give them goals. The results will astonish you.

Once your players are focused and relaxed going into a game, their ability to execute under pressure becomes possible and even probable. The way to know if you are well prepared to execute under game conditions is to practice those conditions. Each day when we end practice (refer to Chapter 9) we create three or four game situations and give the players a plan as to how they can win. We then have our first and second units compete, with the losers running sprints. These situations should be as game-like as possible. Players can *learn* to make game-winning shots and game-winning free throws. The defense can be given the opportunity to make one big stop, or force one turnover to win the game. Whoever wins should celebrate. Create the excitement you normally feel after an actual game. The loser should put this game behind him and prepare for the next game.

Most games are decided in the last two minutes, so we put the score on the scoreboard and play. Every possible game situation comes up during our practices. As a result, when we play in a real game, we know what we want to do. The mental preparation has been developed and our team is confident that we will win. The competition in our practices is intense, and there is pride at stake. The second unit always wants to beat the first team. At the end of these situations, it is also important to bring your team together and remind them that they are "one" team. While competition is good, working together and believing in each other is even more important. The essence of competition is to allow each player to push himself to be the best he can be, and the goal is to make the team the best it can be.

COMMITMENT

I learned a very valuable lesson about coaching and commitment during the 1994-95 season. At that time, I had been the head coach at Bowling Green for seven years. Subsequently, I had the opportunity to enlist the help of a Bowling Green State University professor of sociology, Dr. John Piper. Dr. Piper was an outstanding teacher and was very popular with his students. His specialty was the sociology of sport – a subject which he not only taught at the university but also lectured on frequently around the country. Dr. Piper studied all sports and their effects on our society. He had observed a countless number of teams and coaches and studied their behavior patterns.

Dr. Piper used to enjoy stopping by our Bowling Green practices and watching us prepare for an opponent, and then attend the game to see how well we executed. After a while, I decided to invite Dr. Piper into our locker room to discuss his observations with our players and coaches. As an outstanding motivational speaker, he had everyone's undivided attention for over an hour as he explained his theory of commitment and how it could impact our team.

Dr. Piper directed all of his comments to the team from his wealth of knowledge about athletes' behavior. He explained to them that there are four levels of commitment and that each level you reach allows you to elevate yourself and the people around you to new heights. The four levels are:

- Physical

- Mental

- Emotional

- Spiritual

He explained that many athletes are able to achieve success at the first level. Almost every athlete, especially at the college level, has a certain amount of physical ability and is willing to work hard enough to enjoy some physical success. Most athletes are willing to put in the time and effort physically in order to compete.

The next level, the mental commitment, is a little more difficult to achieve. The mental commitment forces an athlete to commit to working hard even when they don't feel like it. You must prepare yourself mentally and become a student of the game. It is no longer enough just to be fast and jump high; you must know *how* to apply your physical ability to become efficient.

The emotional state is the next level of commitment. This level is the most wide-ranging area we see with players. At the emotional level, the player must be able to control his "fear, his anxiety, his happiness, his sadness, his enthusiasm, his depression." We have all coached players who are either too laid back or too hyper. Working with these types of players to teach them to control their emotions and channel their energies is a big part of coaching. A player who is too laid back during competition has not reached the third level of commitment. He has not learned that it is okay, in fact necessary, to get himself "psyched" to practice and play. He should understand that it is perfectly acceptable behavior to be laid back in a non-competitive situation off the court. But once he crosses the lines on the 94 by 50-foot court, he must be emotionally ready to compete. He should energize himself and say "for the next two hours I am going to be committed: physically, mentally and emotionally focused on being the best I can be."

The same is true for the player who is too hyper. He must be able to relax and focus on controlling his emotions. His goal should still be to be the best he can be; overworking, getting frustrated, and losing his cool will not help the situation.

The fourth level of commitment is spiritual. It is the elusive state that every player and coach wants to reach. It is that mind-set when everyone is able to put the team first at all times. You are looking for that "team spirit" that says:

"No one cares who gets the credit, we just plan on getting the job done."

Whenever you bring highly motivated and goal-oriented people together, it becomes a real challenge to get them to work together. It seems each individual has his own way of reaching his peak performance. There are days, and sometimes weeks, when a team stays totally focused and is able to reach that elusive fourth level of commitment. It is a beautiful thing to observe. The team is playing as if it had one mind, one soul. The term "synergy" best describes this situation, where the whole is greater than the sum of all its parts. Everybody feeds off each other. Everybody accepts things as they are, and knows that the team comes before all personal and individual goals. Every team needs to understand "the goal is to reach Level 4."

COACHING

After listening to Dr. Piper, I invited him to share his observations about the coaches he had studied with me and my staff. I felt that we could learn a lot from his observations. His information proved to be very helpful. Dr. Piper explained that there are three categories of coaches and that almost all coaches fall into one of these categories:

- Practice coach

- Game coach

- Players' coach (i.e., teaching/trusting coach)

Some coaches are great teachers. They are like a professor holding class on the court. The players learn and improve and the team is always well prepared. Other coaches are game coaches and are able to make instinctive adjustments in games. They have a great feel for the game and can easily and calmly communicate their thoughts to their players no matter how stressful the situation. These coaches often win close games because their teams are like them – cool, calm and collected at the end of close games.

The practice coach prepares his team well, but then during the actual contest continues to correct every mistake, like it was practice. I often found myself making corrections under game conditions that I needed to ignore. I should have waited until we got back out on the practice floor to help improve this situation.

Game coaches, on the other hand, rely too frequently on their gut instincts and spend relatively little time teaching the skills of the game and helping players improve in practice. They like to "X and O" the game but not truly develop the individual player. Everyone becomes a pawn in his own personal game of chess.

The best category is the players' coach who prepares his team fully in practice with drills to develop essential skills, with a solid X-and-O game plan, and with a clear vision of how he expects the team to play. However, once the game begins, he trusts that what he has taught them in practice will be executed under game conditions.

If a mistake occurs, the coach should applaud. That's right, he should clap. Dr. Bob Rotella has convinced me that this step is the only logical reaction to a mistake. Dr. John Piper states that the truly great coaches have so much confidence that they believe that once you have prepared your team, questioning or correcting them on the court will only lead to indecision. Given my utmost respect for these renowned professionals, following their advice made perfect sense.

This strategy doesn't mean that you never make corrections or adjustments during a game. Rather, it means that you should be patient with your players and find an appropriate time to address issues that you feel need to be covered. Making adjustments at time-outs and half-time is still necessary. However, I believe *what* you say to your team and *how* you say it will be very different once you commit yourself to clapping for mistakes, such as missed shots, or bad plays. Your players will remain more calm and confident. Over time, you will find that your strategy will pay off in all your close games.

On February 28, 1999, we played Old Dominion in the CAA Tournament Championship Game with an NCAA berth on the line. With seven minutes remaining, we led by 14 points. Old Dominion went on a big run. With only one minute remaining, and the shot clock at three seconds, we led by only one point. What would happen during this next one minute and three seconds is a direct result of believing in what we'd practiced (i.e., the principles advocated by Dr. Rotella and Dr. Piper) and trusting in my players.

First of all, Jason Miskiri, an All CAA First-Team performer, elevated and shot and made a 25-foot jump shot to give us a 4-point lead. Jason was 3 for 16 at the time and had not made a 3-pointer. His shot hit nothing but net. Then our defense held Old Dominion, and it appeared we were about to seal the victory. Instead, Keith Holdan, a remarkably consistent player, made an errant pass that was stolen which immediately led to a fast-break lay-up. Keith, overanxious, reached in and fouled the shooter for a 3-point play. It was now back to a one-point game. Momentum gone. I clapped. My assistants clapped. We were still very upbeat. We told our team that "there was still a lot of basketball to be played and just stay relaxed and confident."

ODU called a time out to set up their press. Enter, Tremaine Price. Tremaine was our back-up point guard. He was also our second best ball handler. The night before, in our semi-final victory, he missed two key free throws that would have iced the game. We were now putting him in to help break the press and possibly shoot two more, "BIG" free throws. ODU pressed and then elected to foul Holdan. It made sense. Holdan had just made a huge mistake. Now he had two free-throws that could put us up by three. Everyone clapped. Holdan nailed them both. ODU scored quickly to cut the lead back to one. Miskiri then hit two free throws, and our defense held. Finally, with six seconds to play, Price was fouled. He was back at the foul line. We are clinging to a 3-point lead. He calmly took a breath, went through his routine, sighted his target, and nailed both of them. Old Dominion shot a desperation three as the buzzer sounded. We won the CAA Title.

Following the game, Miskiri was asked how he felt when he made the big three with one minute remaining. "Did you realize that you were having an awful night shooting, and hadn't made a three-pointer all game?," asked a reporter. Jason responded that he never considered his shooting percentage, and only planned on making the shot. "My coaches have confidence in me, and as a result, I have confidence in myself to take and make the big shot," he responded with a huge smile on his face and the championship net around his neck.

In the locker room, Tremaine Price waited for me to return from a half-hour press conference and thanked me for showing such confidence in him. He was dying to make up for the miss the night before. I was dying to let him. I believed in him and wanted him to know it. I am absolutely convinced that positive reinforcement goes a long way toward building confidence and championship teams. A true testament of teaching, then trusting, your players. This example is just one instance that confirms the value of trust.

EPILOGUE

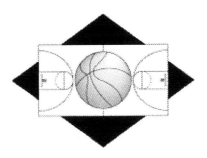

FROM WORST TO FIRST

Do you want to be successful? The answer is obviously yes. On April 1, 1997, I became the head men's basketball coach at George Mason University. The basketball program had just struggled through its seventh consecutive losing season. GMU had finished ninth, dead last, again. The program, the school, and the fans were experiencing tremendous frustration.

How could we turn a program around with all of the losing, when everybody was so down on our players. We had two seniors, returning starters, Demetrius Somerville, out with a broken leg, and Avery Carey, who needed back surgery. Veterans, Nik Mirich, Ahmad Dorsett, Lee Brown, and Leighton Henry as letter winners with a combined scoring average of 10 points per game. We also had Nas Abraham, a transfer from Loyola, who would be eligible in the fall. Seven players. Not exactly the building blocks of a championship-caliber team. Yet, when I accepted the position, I made it clear that winning the conference championship was our goal. At our first team meeting, I asked the players one question, "Do you want to be successful?" Raise your hand. The answer was unanimous. All hands flew up in the air. They wanted to be successful. Then I asked, "Do you know how to be successful, and what it takes to be successful?" I told them that "Success" was a choice. That "Success" had a certain look. Mirich, a 6'10", 240 pound power forward, stood in front of me, wearing a beard, shoulder-length hair, and a head band. His shirt was ripped, and he wore sandals. I told the players that I did not have all the answers, but that my experience had taught me several things. First of all, there are a lot of ways of doing things correctly. We can all have our own way, and they can all be right. However, for us to be successful, we should ask ourselves "Can we have 13 different ways of doing something and can all of us still be successful?" "Can the team function as a unit this way?" The answer to these questions is obviously, "no."

Second, my job as the "head coach" is to choose the way; your job as "players" is to make it work. We are a train running along the same track with me as the conductor. If you trust in me, we can all reach our destination together. I may be wrong at times. I may not always choose the right way. But if we work together in the same direction, we can and we will be successful.

I said that role models are important and that we wanted to be great role models for those youngsters who followed our program. We also wanted to use role models to determine how we would succeed. Just look at several of the top programs in the country – Duke, Carolina, Kentucky. They all carried themselves with great dignity and pride. They looked successful.

I said take a look at Mirich. Would he fit in at those programs? The answer is no. Is there anything wrong with long hair and a beard? The answer is no. Many famous and successful people wore either long hair or a beard or both. But if success had a look, then Mirich would look successful if he were a rock star – not a college basketball player. We stressed to each and every player to get on the same page and work furiously to improve. We began by shaving and cutting our hair and looking like "Joe athlete."

We ordered top-brand Nike shoes, warm ups and athletic gear to enhance our commitment to look like players. We established some short-range goals for our first month, and began working to achieve them. We invited the players to my house for a pizza party and talked to them about what was important for the future development of our program.

We created a vision. Can we be the hardest working team in our conference? Can we be the hardest working team in the country? Do we have hard workers or lazy players? What will we stand for? What will be our *TRADEMARK?* When people speak about George Mason Basketball, will it be with respect?

We spoke about how important it is to play great defense. Anyone can become a great team -defensive player. You just have to want it bad enough. On offense, you must have great shooters, passers, dribblers, and rebounders. On defense, however, you just need the determination to learn how to play defense and then get the job done.

Our underlying theme became "Turning up the heat!" Relentless pressure defense was our vision. We put it on the backs of all our t-shirts and distributed it to our players, coaches, and fans. When we took the floor for practice and game warm-ups, the sound system played the Glenn Frey song, "The Heat is On," all over the arena. It was "our song," and everyone knew its meaning.

In the spring of 1997, George Mason was again picked to finish last in the Colonial Athletic Association. On Sunday, February 28, 1999, we cut down the nets – as CAA Champions. In two short years, we went from worst to first. The excitement surrounding our program was almost too much to believe. The television and newspaper coverage was nonstop for the entire week leading up to the NCAA Tournament. NBC, CBS, ABC, and ESPN cameras and a host of other television networks were on hand at the Patriot Center as the NCAA Selection Show began. We were the cover story on *The Washington Post* sports page the day after Selection Sunday. A color photo of our team announced that we were "Going to the Big Dance!" Two thousand Patriot fans filled our arena as we watched Selection Sunday on a 30-foot wide TV screen hanging from our rafters. The great part is that the excitement will continue to grow for many seasons to come.

ABOUT THE AUTHOR

Jim Larranaga is the head men's basketball coach at George Mason University. Since assuming his present position in 1997, Larranaga has led the Patriots to national prominence. In 1999, he was named Colonial Athletic Association Coach of the Year for guiding George Mason to its first ever CAA regular season title and its second ever berth in the NCAA Tournament.

Prior to his arrival at George Mason, Larranaga achieved a 170-144 mark in an outstanding 11-year career as head men's basketball coach at Bowling Green State University from 1986-'97. Larranaga's 170 wins at Bowling Green are second most in school history, and he was only the second Falcon coach to record consecutive post-season appearances. In 1997 (his last season at Bowling Green), he was named the Mid-American Conference Coach of the Year after leading the Falcons to a 22-10 record and a regular season co-championship.

A 1971 graduate of Providence College where he received a degree in economics, Larranaga was a four-year letterman for the Friars. In his senior season, he was the team captain, leading Providence to a 20-8 record and an NIT appearance. He graduated as the school's fifth all-time leading scorer with 1,258 points.

He began his coaching career at Davidson College where he served as an assistant coach to Terry Holland. Davidson captured three Southern Conference championships and an NIT berth. Doubling as the freshman coach, his teams were 47-12. In 1976, he left Davidson and spent one season as player-coach for the Geronemo Basketball Club in Belgium where his team was 18-10.

He received his first head coaching position in 1977 when he was named to the post at American International College, a Division II program in Springfield, MA. Taking a program which had suffered through five consecutive losing seasons prior to his arrival, Larranaga turned AIC into a winning program in his first year and compiled a 28-25 mark in two seasons from 1977-'79.

In 1979, he was reunited with Holland at the University of Virginia. An assistant coach under Holland for seven seasons from 1979-'86, Larranaga helped the Cavaliers reach the NCAA "Final Four" on two occasions (1981 and 1984), finish in the top five of the AP and UPI polls and average more than 25 victories per season. The Cavaliers were 169-62, won three regular season Atlantic Coast Conference championships, and made four NCAA Tournament appearances.

Widely recognized as a "player's coach," Larranaga has compiled a career record of 245-209 in 16 years as a head coach. His teams are known for their offensive efficiency and their frenetic, pressure defense.

Larranaga and his wife, Liz, have two children—Jay and Jon.